THE GOURMET BARBECUE

THE
GOURMET
BARBECUE

Pip Bloomfield and Annie Mehra

Photography by Peter Johnson

Prima Publishing
P.O. Box 1260KS
Rocklin, CA 95677
(916) 624-5718

Photography: Peter Johnson
Typesetting: Computer Composition of Canada Inc.

Prima Publishing
Rocklin, CA

Published by arrangement with Key Porter Books, Canada

Library of Congress Cataloging-in-Publication Data

Bloomfield, Pip.
    The gourmet barbecue / by Pip Bloomfield and Annie Mehra.
       p.   cm.
    Reprint. Originally published: 1986.
    Includes index.
    ISBN 1-55958-074-7
    1. Barbecue cookery.   I. Mehra, Annie.
III. Title.
TX840.B3B56   1991   91-7512
641.7′6—dc20   CIP

91 92 93 94 RRD 10 9 8 7 6 5 4 3 2 1

Printed in the United States of America

Contents

'For Jennie, Vic and Peter'

Acknowledgments

The authors would like to thank the following people for their help with this book:

Janice Baker
Patricia Cohen
Ivan Haege
Janet Strickland
Julie Wilson

plus all the other family and friends who have assisted.

Special thanks to Doris Cohen

Thanks for the photographic props to:

Appley Hoare Antiques
Mosman NSW

Inini
Neutral Bay Shopping Village
NSW

Peter Johnson

Introduction

This book will show you how to prepare exciting and different meals on your barbecue with a minimum of effort. We hope to convince people that barbecuing is a means of cooking interesting creative food in a convivial atmosphere.

Not all these recipes are designed to be cooked on the barbecue. There are appetizers and dips, vegetables, salads and desserts that can be prepared in advance to let you get on with the task at hand.

With one or two exceptions, you will not need any fancy cooking utensils. All our recipes have been tested on the simplest equipment; therefore, depending on the type of barbecue you have, some of the timings may need to be adjusted.

Our book will provide you with the chance to cook an Indian, Chinese, Australian, Malaysian, West Indian, French, Greek or Italian feast on your barbecue.

Most of the ingredients in this book are readily available. The recipes themselves are easy to follow, and even an inexperienced cook will enjoy discovering them.

It is important to experiment a little. If you love hot spicy food, add a little more chili or cayenne pepper. If you have access to fresh herbs and adore them, be generous with your measurements. Use the recipes as a guideline to bring out your own flair and imagination.

Pip Bloomfield
Annie Mehra

Useful Facts and Figures

All oven temperatures are given in Fahrenheit (°F.) followed by Celsius (°C).

All spoon sizes are level measures of standard measuring spoons.

Where fresh spices and herbs are called for, one-third the amount of dried or ground ingredient may be substituted.

Hints for Barbecuing

Any food you would normally grill in your kitchen can be barbecued. Be careful of anything that softens or crumbles easily as it cooks, and avoid less-tender meats which require long, slow cooking.

Organization is the key to a successful barbecue. Before you start cooking, make sure you have everything within arm's reach (marinades, utensils, sauces). A meal can be ruined if you have to run into the kitchen to collect something you have forgotten.

Allow more food for a barbecue than you would for an indoor meal. Eating outside increases the appetite.

Place your barbecue in a sheltered but not isolated position, so that the smoke, if there is any, will be carried away from your main entertaining area.

When selecting barbecue equipment, you will find that there are many different types available — from the simplest charcoal-fueled hibachi to medium-sized grills to elaborate vented barbecues (some of which have motorized rotisseries, built-in thermometers and covers). Obviously, the latter group is more expensive, but if barbecuing is a way of life for you, then it probably pays to spend the extra money. Today, gas and electric barbecues are popular. They are easier to operate and tidier than the barbecues that burn charcoal and briquettes. When using them, follow the manufacturer's directions.

Keep your barbecue trolley stocked with some indispensable accessories. These include a good pair of insulated gloves or mitts, a saucepan you can place directly on the barbecue, a long-handled bristle (not plastic) basting brush, a wooden spoon, a good pair of long tongs, a flat spatula, a meat thermometer, a couple of hinged wire grills and a roll of aluminum foil.

Briquettes are excellent for barbecuing. They burn for a reasonable length of time and distribute the heat evenly. Firestarters are useful to get the fire alight easily. The simplest way to get a fire going is to shape your charcoal or briquettes into a mound. Place three or four firestarters into the mound and light them. Once your fuel has turned to gray embers, spread them evenly and start cooking. Never try to cook over an open flame.

Kerosene and gasoline should never be used for lighting a fire. They are extremely dangerous and must be kept well away from your barbecue. Always keep sufficient water at hand to douse any unexpected flare-up. For smaller problems, an atomizer is very effective. Always extinguish your fire completely before leaving it.

If you are using wood, choose dry varieties which produce long-lasting coals. Never use a resinous wood such as pine, or it will taint (and in some cases, poison) the food. Oak is ideal. Aromatic woods like hickory or mesquite add a delicious flavor to your barbecue cooking, and lots of fresh herbs thrown straight on the coals are good too.

For a more concentrated heat, make sure the coals are close together. If you require a lower heat, spread them out. To test the heat of your barbecue place your hand above the grill. You should be able to leave it there for 2 or 3 seconds for hot, 4 to 6 seconds for medium-hot, and 7 to 10 seconds for medium-low.

Most outdoor chefs prefer to serve barbecued steaks "rare to medium." They are juicier and tenderer than well-done steaks. Here is a guide to help you cook your steaks.

BARBECUE TIMETABLE	MINUTES PER SIDE		
THICKNESS	RARE	MEDIUM	WELL DONE
1 inch (2.5 cm)	5-6	8-9	10-13
1½ inches (2.5-4 cm)	6-7	10-13	18-20
2 inches (5 cm)	10-13	20-25	30-35

Avoid losing all the good juices by using your finger instead of a knife to test for doneness. For rare, steak is brown on the outside and soft to the touch; medium is slightly firmer but springs back when touched; well-done steak is firm throughout.

Hints for Food

If food has been refrigerated, it is advisable to bring it back to room temperature before barbecuing or it may burn on the outside and be raw in the middle.

Never use a fork to turn meat as it punctures the flesh and you lose valuable juices. These can also cause flare-ups in the fire. Always use tongs or spatulas.

A few tips for marinating:

• Always use a glass or ceramic dish for marinating your food. Metal can taint.

• Turn the food a few times while it is marinating so the flavors are absorbed.

• When basting food during cooking, never pour on the marinade or baste. Always brush it on or you will cause flare-ups. Keep the marinade in a jug or small bowl to make basting easy.

• Always oil your grill, hotplate or foil very well to prevent food from sticking.

Appetizers

Appetizers are a delicious treat to kick off your barbecue. Serve them while waiting for the main meal to cook to take the edge off your guests' hunger and allow everyone to enjoy the barbecue more.

Some of these recipes can be used as a main course if you like. Just double the recipe.

If you don't wish to serve a first course, use your appetizers as accompaniments to a main meal or serve a few dishes together with a salad or two.

SKEWERED OYSTERS

Serves 4 to 8

2 tbsp.	butter
1	clove garlic, crushed
40	small mushrooms
	Salt
	Freshly ground black pepper
1 tbsp.	finely chopped fresh parsley
48	fresh oysters, shucked
8	bamboo skewers, soaked in water for 1 hour

Melt butter in a large frying pan. Add crushed garlic and sauté for 1 to 2 minutes. Add mushrooms, salt and pepper. Cook for 1 to 2 minutes. Toss in parsley and cook for 30 seconds. Remove mushrooms from pan.

Thread 6 oysters, alternating with 5 mushrooms, on each bamboo skewer.

Place on grill over low coals. Cook 1 to 2 minutes, turning often.

SIZZLING OYSTERS

Serves 4

¼ cup	fresh parsley, finely chopped
4 strips	bacon, cooked until crisp then finely chopped
	Freshly ground black pepper
	Hot pepper sauce
2 tbsp.	grated Gruyère cheese
24	oysters in their half shells
4	lemon wedges

Combine parsley, bacon, pepper, hot pepper sauce and Gruyère cheese. Place oysters on grill over hot coals. Cook until they begin to sizzle in their shells. Sprinkle mixture on oysters. Serve with lemon wedges.

OYSTERS IN TANGY BBQ SAUCE

Serves 4

| 24 | fresh oysters in half shells |

SAUCE

1 cup	catsup
2/3 cup	water
6 tbsp.	lemon juice
1/4 cup	vegetable oil
2 tbsp.	Worcestershire sauce
1 tbsp.	brown sugar
8 drops	hot pepper sauce
1/4 tsp.	dry mustard
1 tsp.	garlic salt
1	onion, finely chopped

Combine all sauce ingredients in a small saucepan. Simmer for 5 minutes over low heat, stirring often.

Spoon sauce over oysters. Place oysters in their half shells on barbecue grill above an even bed of glowing coals, or place to one side where the heat is not as intense.

Heat the oysters about 3 minutes or until the sauce sizzles. Serve immediately.

DATE AND BACON SKEWERS

Makes 12 appetizers

½ cup	water
½ cup	fresh orange juice
½ cup	lightly packed brown sugar
1	grated zest of orange
¼ cup	red wine
1 inch	cinnamon stick
3	whole cloves
¼ tsp.	ground nutmeg
	Pinch salt
24	pitted dates
4	bacon strips, cut into thirds
12	bamboo skewers, soaked in water for 1 hour

The day before the barbecue, place water, orange juice, brown sugar, orange zest, red wine, cinnamon stick, cloves, nutmeg and salt in a saucepan. Bring to a boil, reduce heat and simmer for 10 minutes.

Place dates in a bowl. Pour orange juice mixture over dates. Cover and let cool. Refrigerate for 12 to 24 hours.

Remove dates from bowl. Discard marinade. Wrap 2 dates in each piece of bacon. Skewer with bamboo stick. Repeat, using all dates and bacon.

Place on oiled barbecue grill at a medium distance from the coals. Cook for 6 to 8 minutes or until bacon is crisp.

RUMAKI

Marinate on the day

Makes 8 appetizers

1 lb.	chicken livers
6 strips	bacon
10 oz. can	whole water chestnuts
8	bamboo skewers, soaked in water for 1 hour

MARINADE

¼ cup	soy sauce
¼ cup	brown sugar
2	cloves garlic, crushed
2 tbsp.	dry sherry
1 tsp.	freshly grated ginger
2 tbsp.	sesame oil

Wash chicken livers thoroughly. Drain on paper towel. Trim and cut livers in half and set aside.

In a large bowl, combine marinade ingredients. Add livers, making sure each piece is covered by the marinade. Marinate for at least 1 hour. Drain livers. Reserve marinade.

Cut bacon into small pieces. Drain water chestnuts. Thread a water chestnut, then a chicken liver, then a piece of bacon on each skewer. Repeat the procedure until all the ingredients are used up.

Place on barbecue grill over hot coals. Cook, basting frequently with the marinade, 10 to 12 minutes, turning often. When done, baste generously with the marinade and serve immediately.

TAPENADE

Makes 2 cups

A delicious Mediterranean spread.

1½ cups	large black olives, pitted
¼ cup	drained capers
2	cloves garlic, peeled and coarsely chopped
2 2-oz. cans	anchovy fillets in oil, drained
1 tsp.	Dijon mustard
¼ cup	olive oil
	Freshly ground black pepper
	Dash lemon juice
2 tbsp.	chopped fresh parsley
	Milk

Soak anchovies in milk for 5 to 10 minutes.

Place pitted olives in blender or food processor. Add remaining ingredients. Process until smooth.

Serve with hot crusty French bread, with raw vegetables or with buttered Melba toast (page 17).

NOTE:
You can store the tapenade for up to three months in the refrigerator. Place in several small sterilized glass jars. Pack tapenade firmly. Cover with a thin layer of olive oil and screw on airtight lids.

Rumaki (p. 5) and Tapenade

EGGPLANT "CAVIAR"

A spread rather than a dip, this is a poor man's version of caviar.

1	large eggplant
2	medium onions, finely chopped
1	green pepper, finely chopped
1	stalk celery, finely chopped
1/4 cup	olive oil
	Salt
	Freshly ground black pepper
1	clove garlic, crushed

In a 350°F. (180°C) oven, bake whole eggplant for 25 to 30 minutes or until soft. When cool, peel and chop the flesh.

Sauté onions, green pepper and celery in olive oil until golden brown. Add sautéed vegetables and the oil to chopped cooked eggplant. Mash or blend. Add salt, pepper and garlic and stir well. Serve with hot buttered toast.

BASIC MAYONNAISE

Makes 1¼ cups

3	egg yolks at room temperature
1/4 tsp.	salt
	Pinch white pepper
1 tsp.	Dijon mustard
2 tbsp.	lemon juice
1 1/4 cups	vegetable oil

Beat egg yolks until pale and creamy. Add salt and pepper, mustard and 1 tsp. of lemon juice. Beat continuously until mayonnaise begins to thicken.

Add oil drop by drop, beating constantly as mixture continues to thicken. Add half the remaining lemon juice. Add the rest of the oil in a fine, steady stream until it is well absorbed and the mayonnaise is creamy. Add the rest of the lemon juice and season to taste.

Store mayonnaise in the refrigerator.

Indian Leg of Lamb (p. 75)

SHRIMP IN PIZZAZ PLUM SAUCE

Serves 6

2 lb.   jumbo shrimp

MARINADE

¼ cup	dry white wine
2 tbsp.	finely chopped fresh parsley
3	cloves garlic, crushed
1 tbsp.	finely chopped fresh ginger root

PLUM SAUCE

14 oz. can	purple plums
½ cup	port
1	bay leaf
4	whole cloves
2 tbsp.	red wine vinegar
1 tbsp.	cornstarch
1 tbsp.	cold water
	Pinch salt

The day before the barbecue, shell the shrimp, leaving tails intact. Remove spinal veins.

Combine ingredients for marinade. Add shrimp. Cover and refrigerate for 24 hours.

The day of the barbecue, make the plum sauce. Drain the liquid from the plums and put it in a saucepan. Reserve plums. To the saucepan add port, bay leaf, cloves and wine vinegar. Simmer for 5 minutes.

Blend cornstarch with cold water. Stir into sauce. Cook over low heat, stirring with a wooden spoon, until sauce becomes clear and thickens. Strain and add salt.

Place plums in blender or food processor. Process until puréed. Add purée to sauce.

Before barbecue, remove shrimp from marinade. Reserve marinade. Place shrimp in a well-oiled, hinged grill basket, or if they are large enough, place them on the barbecue grill. Cook above medium-hot coals for 3 to 4 minutes on each side, brushing frequently with the marinade. Turn shrimp only once during cooking.

Remove shrimp from barbecue. Serve with plum sauce.

BRIE MOUSSE

Serves 6

1 envelope	unflavored gelatin
½ cup	cold milk
½ lb.	ripe Brie cheese, finely chopped
2 tbsp.	pimento, drained and chopped
2 tbsp.	finely chopped fresh chives
2 tbsp.	finely chopped fresh parsley
2 tsp.	capers, drained
½ tsp.	paprika
¼ tsp.	cayenne pepper
2 tsp.	prepared English mustard
1 tsp.	salt
½ cup	whipping cream
1	egg white
	Lemon juice
	Freshly ground black pepper
1 2-cup	mold

In a heavy saucepan, combine gelatin and milk. Cook over low heat, stirring with a wooden spoon, until gelatin is dissolved. Add cheese and stir until cheese is melted.

Remove from heat. Add pimento, chives, parsley, capers, paprika, cayenne pepper, mustard and salt. Let cool.

While mixture is cooling, whip cream. In a separate bowl, whip egg white until soft peaks form. With a large metal spoon, carefully fold whipped cream, then egg white into the cooled cheese mixture. When cream and egg white are mixed throughout, turn mixture into the greased mold. Cover and chill for several hours, or until firm.

Place mold in hot water for a few seconds. Unmold on a serving dish and surround with a variety of crackers.

Just before serving, squeeze a little lemon juice over the mousse and grind a little pepper on top.

SHRIMP AND PINE NUTS ENTRÉE

1	small onion, finely chopped
1 tbsp.	butter
1 lb.	uncooked shrimp, peeled, de-veined and finely chopped
¼ cup	pine nuts
1 tbsp.	lemon juice
	Additional lemon juice
½ cup	Basic Mayonnaise (page 9)
2 tbsp.	finely chopped fresh parsley
3 or 4	shallots, finely chopped
½ tsp.	cayenne pepper
	Pinch paprika to garnish
	Salt to taste

Sauté onion in butter until transparent. Add shrimp and pine nuts. Sauté for 1 minute. Add lemon juice and cook for another minute.

Remove shrimp, onions and nuts with a slotted spoon. Cool. Add additional lemon juice to taste.

Fold shrimp mixture into mayonnaise. Add parsley, shallots and cayenne pepper.

Spoon mixture into a decorative bowl. Garnish with paprika. Cover with plastic wrap and refrigerate. Spread on crackers to serve.

SPICY ALMONDS

2 tbsp.	vegetable oil
½ lb.	blanched almonds
1 tsp.	salt
¼ tsp.	cumin powder
1 tsp.	chili powder
1 tsp.	garam masala

In hot oil over medium heat, stir-fry the blanched almonds until they turn a pale golden color.

Quickly remove the nuts with a slotted spoon and drain on paper towels. Sprinkle with salt, cumin, chili and garam masala.

Dips

Dips are easy to make. Serve a couple when barbecuing to relieve your guests' hunger.

There is an enormous variety of things to dunk into dips: crudités (raw vegetables), tortilla chips, fresh crusty bread, Melba toast, bread sticks, cheese crackers and pita bread.

Some dips can be refrigerated for a couple of days in an airtight container. Just allow them to come back to room temperature before eating. Some dips should not be refrigerated, as they become solid.

MIDDLE EASTERN DIP

2	shallots, finely chopped
2	cloves garlic, crushed
2 tbsp.	olive oil
2 tsp.	curry powder
2 tbsp.	seasoned pepper
2 tbsp.	tomato paste diluted in equal amount of water
2 tbsp.	lemon juice
1 tbsp.	apricot jam
½ cup	Basic Mayonnaise (page 9)

Cook shallots and garlic in oil. When soft, add curry powder, pepper, tomato paste, lemon juice and jam. Simmer for 4 to 5 minutes.

Place in a blender and process until smooth or press through a sieve. Let cool. Add the mayonnaise. Mix well. Chill.

Serve with crudités.

GUACAMOLE

2	large ripe avocados, peeled and chopped
1	medium tomato, peeled, seeded and chopped
½	onion, finely chopped
1	clove garlic, crushed
½ tsp.	salt
1 tbsp.	lemon juice
¼ tsp.	chili powder
2 tbsp.	chopped fresh coriander
1 tbsp.	chopped crisply cooked bacon

Place all ingredients except bacon in the food processor. Blend until smooth. Remove from blender and stir in bacon. Serve with corn chips or Mexican tostaditas (available in gourmet shops).

BAGNA CAUDA

This creamy hot garlic dip is excellent with crudités.

⅔ cup	whipping cream
¼ cup	olive oil
2 tbsp.	butter
6 to 8	cloves garlic, crushed
2-oz. can	anchovies, drained and pounded in a mortar
¼ lb.	finely chopped walnuts
	Black pepper

Heat butter and oil very gently in a shallow, heavy pan. Add garlic and cook for 2 minutes. Remove pan from heat and stir in anchovies and walnuts.

Return the pan to low heat and stir until anchovies are well blended into the sauce. Season with black pepper. Add cream over low heat.

Keep the dip warm by pouring it into a fondue or earthenware pot and placing over low heat. Be careful not to let the sauce boil. Stir often.

Serve with crudités. Use small forks to dip the vegetables into the hot sauce.

CRUDITÉS   Use any of these cut in bite-sized pieces:

Celery
Green beans
Broccoli
Carrots
Cauliflower
Cucumber

Mushrooms
Radishes
Red or green pepper
Snow peas
Zucchini

GOURMET CHEESE DIP

¼ lb.	Cheddar cheese, grated
¼ lb.	Danish blue cheese, crumbled
¼ lb.	Port Salut cheese, cut in small pieces
¼ lb.	cream cheese, cut in small pieces
¼ lb.	sour cream
1 tbsp.	sherry
12 drops	hot pepper sauce
2	small cloves garlic, crushed

Place all ingredients in a blender or food processor. Process until the mixture is light and creamy.

Serve at room temperature with crudités or Melba toast triangles (recipe follows).

HORSERADISH DIP

Makes about 1½ cups

8 oz.	cream cheese
¼ cup	sour cream
¼ cup	prepared horseradish
2 tbsp.	chopped fresh parsley
1 tbsp.	grated onion
4 tsp.	lemon juice

Combine all ingredients. Blend well and serve with bread sticks.

MELBA TOAST TRIANGLES

Makes 40 pieces of Melba toast

10	very thin slices white bread

Preheat oven to 300°F. (150°C).

Remove crusts from bread. Cut each slice twice diagonally so each slice makes 4 triangles. Place triangles on a baking tray. Bake in oven for 20 minutes.

Turn triangles over. Increase heat to 350°F. (180°C) and bake for 10 minutes more, or until triangles are golden brown. Let cool on rack.

SALMON DIP

8³/₄-oz. can	red salmon (not pink)
¹/₄ cup	mayonnaise
	Juice of ¹/₂ lemon
¹/₂	onion, finely chopped
¹/₂	sweet red pepper, finely chopped
¹/₂	clove garlic, crushed
¹/₂	stalk celery, very finely chopped
2 to 3 sprigs	fresh dill
	Salt
	Freshly ground black pepper
	Fresh dill for garnish

Blend all ingredients except garnish in a food processor or by hand. Cover and chill. Garnish with sprigs of dill and serve with corn chips or celery sticks.

INDIAN YOGURT DIP AND PAPPADUMS

1 tsp.	cumin seeds
2 cups	plain yogurt
2 tbsp.	finely chopped fresh coriander
1 tbsp.	lemon juice
	Salt
½ tsp.	cayenne pepper
24	pappadums (available at Indian grocery stores)

Place cumin seeds in a heavy frying pan. Do not use oil or butter. Over medium heat, toast seeds until fragrant. When toasted, grind seeds to a fine powder.

Put yogurt in a medium-sized bowl. Add ground cumin seeds, coriander, lemon juice, salt and cayenne pepper. Blend thoroughly. Cover and chill.

To cook pappadums: follow the instructions on the package. Keep warm in the oven. Serve with dip.

HOT CRAB DIP

10 oz.	fresh or canned crab meat, drained
8 oz.	cream cheese
1 tbsp.	cream
½ tsp.	chili powder
2 tbsp.	finely chopped onion
¼ tsp.	salt

Preheat oven to 350°F. (180°C).

Blend all ingredients together in a food processor or by hand. Pour into a small ovenproof casserole dish or ramekins and bake for 25 minutes. Serve with French bread or crackers.

Seafood

Always choose very fresh fish. Fresh fish have bright eyes and the flesh is firm and moist, with no overpowering fishy odor.

If you intend to cook a fish you have just caught, clean it thoroughly. Rub salt into the gutted cavity, then rinse well.

To marinate a whole fish, make a few diagonal incisions in two or three places at regular intervals on each side of the fish to allow the marinade to penetrate.

Never overcook fish. The fish is ready when the flesh becomes opaque and flakes easily. Fish takes very little time to cook, so if you are planning to have a varied menu, leave the fish until last so you can give it your complete attention.

If you use a marinade, cook the fish carefully: the marinade weakens the fish and makes it more likely to fall apart. Use a hinged wire grill or place the fish in foil if necessary.

Wrapping fish completely in foil will result in steamed or baked fish. Open foil "boats" also work very well with fish. Oil the foil well on the shiny side before cooking.

Cook fish over a moderate, not hot, fire.

You can stuff whole fish with dried or fresh herbs and spices. Fennel, garlic, orange and lemon peel are particularly good with fish.

Shrimp and prawns do not have to be peeled before going on the barbecue. If you do peel them, remember to remove the spinal vein. Shrimp are best when marinated first.

Large, firm-fleshed fish that have been skinned, boned and cut into cubes are ideal for skewer cooking.

JOHN DORY GRIBICHE

Serves 4

8	ocean perch fillets
4 tsp.	butter
	Fresh dill for garnish

MARINADE

1 cup	dry white wine
½ cup	olive oil
2 tbsp.	white vinegar
	Juice of 1 lemon
3	cloves garlic
2 tbsp.	freshly chopped parsley
1 tbsp.	finely chopped fresh lemon thyme (or ordinary fresh thyme)
	Salt
	Freshly ground black pepper

GRIBICHE

5	hard-boiled egg yolks
	Salt
	Freshly ground black pepper
¼ cup	olive oil
1 tbsp.	tarragon vinegar
1 tsp.	Dijon mustard
1 tsp.	finely chopped fresh dill
1 tsp.	finely chopped fresh tarragon
1 tsp.	finely chopped fresh chives
1 tsp.	capers, drained
2	medium-sized gherkins, chopped
1 tbsp.	chopped fresh parsley
2	hard-boiled egg whites

Wash and pat fillets dry. Place fish in a glass or ceramic dish.

Mix marinade ingredients together in a bowl. Pour marinade over fish and leave for 2 hours, turning fish once.

To make gribiche, place the cooked egg yolks in a bowl with salt and pepper. Mash well. Add oil drop by drop, then slowly add vinegar, stirring constantly with a wooden spoon.

Keep sauce creamy by adding a little lukewarm water if necessary. Stir in the mustard. Add dill, tarragon, chives, capers, gherkins and parsley. Fold in whites of eggs with metal spoon. Adjust seasoning if necessary.

To barbecue, cut four squares of aluminum foil. Put 2 fillets on shiny side of each square and spoon a little of the marinade over the fish. Then add a pat of butter to each and seal.

Barbecue fish parcels for 5 to 8 minutes. Do not turn over. Remove fish, garnish with dill and serve with warm gribiche.

KINGFISH IN COINTREAU

Serves 6

| 6 2-lb. | kingfish cutlets |
| | Freshly ground black pepper |

MARINADE

	Grated zest of ½ lemon
	Grated zest of ½ orange
	Juice of 1 orange
	Juice of 1 lemon
¼ cup	Cointreau
	Salt

The day before the barbecue, place kingfish in a glass or ceramic dish.

Combine marinade ingredients and pour over fish. Cover with plastic wrap and marinate overnight in the refrigerator.

Remove fish from marinade, reserving marinade. Season fish with black pepper, then place on grill over hot coals. Cook 2 to 3 minutes on each side, basting often with marinade.

CARIBBEAN SNAPPER

Serves 4

4	snapper fillets
	Salt
	Fresh lime or lemon juice
2 tbsp.	toasted slivered almonds for garnish

MARINADE

2 tsp.	vegetable oil
4	tiny fresh red chilies, chopped or
1/2 tsp.	sambal oelek
2	cloves garlic, finely chopped
1 tbsp.	grated fresh ginger root
1 cup	plain yogurt
	Salt

Rinse fish well. Pat dry. Rub with a little salt and lime juice. Make 3 or 4 diagonal incisions in fillets and place them on a double layer of aluminum foil.

Heat vegetable oil in a heavy frying pan. When oil is hot, add chilies or sambal oelek, garlic and ginger. Fry gently until fragrant. Remove from heat. Cool slightly and stir in yogurt a little at a time. Add salt to taste.

Spread yogurt mixture on both sides of fillets, working with your fingers so the marinade enters the incisions. Wrap fish loosely in foil. Let stand at room temperature for at least 1 hour.

Place foil-wrapped fish on hot grill above medium-hot coals. Cook 10 to 15 minutes. Unwrap top of foil and cook 5 more minutes, until fish flakes easily. Garnish with toasted almond slivers.

FROGS' LEGS WITH AÏOLI

Serves 4 to 6

| 12 pairs | frogs' legs, skinned |

MARINADE

⅔ cup	olive oil
⅓ cup	dry white wine
1	clove garlic, crushed
	Salt
	Freshly ground black pepper

AÏOLI (GARLIC MAYONNAISE)

3 to 4	cloves garlic, crushed
½ tsp.	salt
2	egg yolks at room temperature
2 tbsp.	lemon juice
½ tsp.	Dijon mustard
1¼ cups	vegetable oil
	Dash white pepper

Put the frogs' legs in a ceramic or glass dish. Combine the marinade ingredients and pour over the frogs' legs. Marinate for about 40 minutes.

To make aïoli, crush garlic with salt in a large bowl. Add egg yolks and whisk until smooth. Add lemon juice and mustard and whisk again. Begin to add oil drop by drop, whisking all the time, until mayonnaise begins to thicken; then add remaining oil in a thin steady stream, whisking constantly. If aïoli becomes too thick, add a few drops of warm water while whisking. Season to taste with white pepper.

Drain the frogs' legs, reserving marinade. Put legs in a hinged wire grill basket and cook over low coals 5 to 6 minutes on each side, basting often with the marinade. Serve with aïoli.

AROMATIC MULLET WITH FENNEL

Serves 4

4 2-lb.   mullet or trout fillets

MARINADE

	Juice of 2 lemons
¼ cup	olive oil
¼ cup	chopped fennel bulb
½ bunch	fresh parsley, coarsely chopped
	Freshly ground black pepper
¼ cup	Pernod

Clean and dry fillets. Make 2 or 3 shallow incisions on both sides of each fillet. Place fillets in a shallow ceramic or glass dish.

Mix marinade ingredients together. Pour marinade over fish and leave in a cool place for 3 hours. Do not refrigerate.

Place fillets on foil. Pour a little of the marinade onto each fillet. Wrap foil around fish.

Barbecue foil-wrapped fillets for 10 minutes. Do not turn them over.

Annie's Special Spicy Chicken (p. 54)

BARBECUED LOBSTER WITH PISTACHIO BUTTER

Serves 4

2 2-lb.	green lobsters or 4 lobster tails

PISTACHIO BUTTER

2 tbsp.	shelled pistachio nuts
	Few drops water
1/4 cup	unsalted butter, softened
	Salt

BASTE

1/2 cup	butter, melted
2 tsp.	lemon juice
	Salt and pepper

To make pistachio butter: place the shelled pistachio nuts in boiling water for a few seconds. Drain and rinse under cold water. Remove skins by pressing the nuts hard between your thumb and forefinger. Pound nuts in a mortar and pestle. Add a few drops of water, then stir in softened butter. Add salt to taste.

Shape butter into a roll. Wrap in waxed paper and chill.

Split lobsters in half lengthwise. Remove and discard the intestine, stomach and gills. Break the claws, remove flesh and add to lobster flesh in the shell.

Combine butter, lemon juice, salt and pepper. Brush lobster with baste and barbecue shell-side down over gentle heat for 15 to 20 minutes. If you are using tails only, cook for 10 to 15 minutes. Serve with a pat of pistachio butter on top.

Barbecued Lobster with Pistachio Butter
King Crabs with Fresh Tomato and Herb Sauce (p. 28)

KING CRABS WITH FRESH TOMATO AND HERB SAUCE

Serves 6

2 lbs.	fresh king crabs

SAUCE

2	onions, finely chopped
2 tbsp.	olive oil
1	carrot, finely chopped
1	clove garlic, crushed
3 lbs.	tomatoes, skinned and quartered
1/4 cup	tomato paste
1 tbsp.	chopped fresh basil
1 tbsp.	chopped fresh parsley
1 tsp.	chopped fresh oregano
1 tsp.	chopped fresh marjoram
2	bay leaves
	Salt and pepper
1 tbsp.	granulated sugar
1 tbsp.	dry white wine

BASTE

2 tbsp.	olive oil
1/2 cup	butter
1/4 cup	finely chopped fresh parsley
1	clove garlic, crushed
1/4 cup	lemon juice
1 tbsp.	Dijon mustard
	Pinch salt
	Freshly ground black pepper

To make sauce, in a heavy saucepan, sauté onions in olive oil until soft. Add the rest of the sauce ingredients. Bring to the boil. Reduce heat. Simmer for 30 minutes.

To make baste, heat olive oil in a frying pan gently for 1 or 2 minutes. Add butter in small pieces and stir. Remove from heat. Stir in parsley, garlic, lemon juice, mustard, salt and pepper. Mix well.

Place crabs on grill above medium-hot coals. Brush with baste and turn occasionally.

The crabs should be ready in 15 to 20 minutes. Crack crabs open and serve with sauce.

GARLIC AND CHILI PRAWNS

Serves 4

1 1/2 lbs.	raw prawns or large shrimp
1 1/2 tsp.	sambal oelek
3	cloves garlic, chopped
1 cup	vegetable oil
1 tsp.	salt

Shell prawns carefully, leaving tails intact. Remove vein with a sharp knife. Wash prawns under cold running water and dry thoroughly with paper towels. Place in a deep glass or ceramic bowl.

Combine sambal oelek, garlic and half the oil in a blender. Blend at high speed until well mixed. Stir in the remaining oil and salt.

Pour oil mixture over prawns, turning them to make sure they are well coated. Cover and marinate in the refrigerator for at least 4 hours. Drain prawns and reserve marinade.

When barbecue coals have burned down to a white ash, set the prawns on the barbecue grill close to the heat. Cook 2 to 3 minutes on each side, brushing with reserved marinade, until prawns are firm and pink. Do not overcook.

TROUT WITH MACADAMIA BUTTER

Serves 4

4 1-lb.	trout
¼ cup	olive oil
	Salt and pepper

MACADAMIA BUTTER

⅛ lb.	unsalted macadamia nuts, toasted
	A few drops cold water
½ cup	unsalted butter

To prepare butter, pound the toasted macadamia nuts to a paste with the water. Add butter. Place on a sheet of waxed paper and shape into a roll. Chill for 2 to 3 hours in refrigerator.

Clean and wash trout thoroughly, leaving heads intact. Pat dry with paper towels. Brush trout with olive oil and season to taste. Place on preheated, oiled barbecue grill over hot coals and cook for about 6 minutes on each side. Serve with a pat of macadamia butter on top.

SOLE ROMESCO

Serves 4

4	fillets of sole
½ cup	all-purpose flour
	Salt and pepper
½ cup	oil or clarified butter

SAUCE

2	tomatoes, peeled, seeded and chopped
4	dried chili peppers, seeded and chopped
10	hazelnuts, toasted
3	cloves garlic, chopped
2 tbsp.	chopped fresh mint
½ tsp.	salt
¼ cup	olive oil
¼ cup	dry sherry
2 tbsp.	white vinegar
	Chopped parsley

To make sauce: in a blender or food processor, blend tomatoes, chilies, hazelnuts, garlic, mint and salt. Add half the olive oil, drop by drop, until mixture is thick. With the motor still running, add the rest of the oil in a steady stream. Turn off motor. Stir in sherry and vinegar. Set aside.

Wash and dry the sole. Combine flour, salt and pepper. Dust fillets with seasoned flour and dip in oil or butter.

Place fillets on a hot barbecue grill. After 2 or 3 minutes, turn very carefully with a metal spatula. After another 2 or 3 minutes, turn the fish again.

While fish is cooking, pour sauce in a bowl and sprinkle with parsley. Serve spooned over piping hot fillets.

INDIAN PERCH

Serves 4

4 1½-lb.	perch or snapper fillets or snapper steaks
2 tbsp.	lemon juice
1½ tsp.	salt

MARINADE

1	small onion, coarsely chopped
1	small piece fresh ginger root, peeled and sliced
2	cloves garlic
1 tsp.	turmeric
1 tsp.	curry powder
4	dried chilies, chopped
	Pinch ground cinnamon
	Pinch ground cloves
1 tbsp.	vegetable oil
1 tbsp.	water

Rinse fish well and pat dry. With a sharp knife, cut diagonal slashes in flesh. Rub fish with lemon juice and salt. Place fish on a double thickness of aluminum foil and set aside.

Place all marinade ingredients in a blender. Blend to make a smooth paste. Rub paste into fish. If any paste remains, spoon over fish.

Wrap fish in the aluminum foil and let sit for 1 hour.

Place wrapped fish on barbecue grill over hot coals. Cook 10 minutes. Turn fish over carefully and cook another 7 minutes. Open foil to let some of the juices evaporate and cook a further 3 to 4 minutes. Serve.

MUSTARD SHRIMP

Serves 4

1 lb.	raw large shrimp or prawns

MARINADE

¼ cup	prepared Dijon mustard
2 tbsp.	water
2 tbsp.	brown sugar
2 tbsp.	prepared horseradish
1 tbsp.	white wine vinegar
1½ tsp.	vegetable oil
	Salt

Shell shrimp, leaving tails intact. Remove spinal vein with the point of a sharp knife.

In a glass or ceramic bowl, combine marinade ingredients. Add shrimp and toss. Cover with plastic wrap and chill for several hours.

Drain shrimp, reserving marinade.

Place shrimp on well-oiled grill over medium-hot coals. Grill for 6 minutes. Turn, then baste twice with reserved marinade and cook 4 to 5 minutes more.

FRESH TUNA WITH LEMON DILL HOLLANDAISE

Serves 4

1 lb.	fresh tuna fillets or
	large salmon fillets
2 tbsp.	olive oil
	Freshly ground black pepper
	Salt

LEMON DILL HOLLANDAISE

4	egg yolks
	Juice of 1 lemon
1 cup	butter, softened
2 tbsp.	snipped fresh dill

To make hollandaise: in the top of a double boiler, over simmering water, beat together the egg yolks and lemon juice. Continue beating until sauce becomes thick and creamy. Remove from heat and cool slightly.

Thoroughly stir in butter a little at a time. Beat until smooth. Fold in dill and set aside to cool.

Cut tuna fillets into large slices. Brush slices with some of the olive oil and season with pepper and salt.

Place fish on a well-oiled barbecue grill over hot coals. Sear the fish for 1 minute. Turn carefully with a spatula. Brush again with oil and sear for another minute. Tuna flesh should turn opaque on the outside but remain a little raw in the middle. (Tuna is traditionally served raw as a Japanese delicacy, so don't worry if you find it is not cooked all the way through.) If you prefer tuna well done, cook for 2 minutes each side, turning once. Baste constantly with olive oil to prevent fish from drying out.

Just before serving, beat hollandaise again to make sure it is still smooth. Serve with tuna fillets.

ORANGE SALMON

Serves 4

4	salmon fillets

MARINADE

2 tbsp.	butter
1	medium onion, finely chopped
1/2 tsp.	dry mustard
1/4 cup	soft brown sugar
	Pinch ground cloves
1/4 cup	orange juice concentrate
1/4 cup	fresh lemon juice
1 tbsp.	catsup
1/4 tsp.	salt
2 tbsp.	brandy

Rinse and dry fish. Make 2 or 3 diagonal incisions in each fish fillet.

In a small saucepan, melt butter over gentle heat. Add onion and sauté until transparent. Add mustard, brown sugar and cloves. Stir together orange juice and lemon juice. Add to saucepan; then stir in catsup and salt. Bring to a boil. Reduce heat and simmer for 10 minutes, stirring often with a wooden spoon.

Add brandy and remove from heat. Place each fillet on shiny side of a square of aluminum foil. Pour marinade over fish then seal the foil. Let stand at room temperature for 1 hour.

Place foil-wrapped fish on grill over hot coals. Cook 5 to 8 minutes. (Do not turn.) Remove fish from foil and serve with marinade.

OYSTER-TOPPED COD STEAKS

Serves 4

4	cod steaks
1/2 cup	softened butter
1/4 cup	lemon juice
	Salt
	Caviar and fresh basil for garnish

SAUCE

2 tbsp.	sour cream
1 tbsp.	red caviar
2 tsp.	lemon juice
	Freshly ground black pepper
6 to 8 drops	hot pepper sauce
12	fresh whole oysters

To make sauce, stir together sour cream, caviar, lemon juice, black pepper and hot pepper sauce. Fold in the oysters. Set aside.

Cut four pieces of aluminum foil. Butter the shiny side of the foil. Place each cutlet on a piece of foil. Over each cutlet, sprinkle lemon juice and salt.

Wrap the fish, making sure there is only one layer of foil around it. Seal loosely. Place wrapped fish on barbecue grill over medium-hot coals and cook for 10 minutes on each side.

Open foil. Place fish on individual plates and spoon a dollop of oyster sauce on each cutlet. Garnish with red caviar and basil leaves.

OCEAN PERCH RÉMOULADE

Serves 4

4	ocean perch fillets
1 tbsp.	finely chopped fresh tarragon

MARINADE

1 cup	dry white wine
½ cup	olive oil
	Juice of ½ lemon
2	cloves garlic, crushed
2 tbsp.	finely chopped fresh parsley
	Freshly ground black pepper
1 tsp.	finely chopped fresh chervil

RÉMOULADE

1 cup	Basic Mayonnaise (page 9)
2 tbsp.	finely chopped sweet gherkins
1 tbsp.	Dijon mustard
1 tbsp.	capers, drained and mashed
1 tbsp.	finely chopped fresh parsley
½ tsp.	finely chopped fresh chervil
½ tsp.	finely chopped fresh tarragon
1 tsp.	anchovy paste

Rinse and pat fillets dry. Make 2 or 3 small incisions in each fillet. Place fillets in shallow ceramic or glass dish. Mix marinade ingredients together and pour over fish. Sprinkle with tarragon. Let marinate for at least 1 hour.

To make rémoulade, combine all ingredients in a large bowl. Mix well and store, covered, in refrigerator until ready to use.

Drain fish, reserving marinade. Wrap fillets loosely in individual pieces of foil, adding a spoonful of marinade to each.

Cook on a grill over hot coals for 8 to 10 minutes. Turn parcels over and cook a further 8 to 10 minutes. Serve with rémoulade.

FRESH SALMON WITH RUSSIAN MAYONNAISE

Serves 4

2 lbs.   fresh salmon or rainbow trout

RUSSIAN MAYONNAISE

¼ cup   Basic Mayonnaise (page 9)
1 tbsp.   red caviar
½ tsp.   dry mustard
½ tsp.   Worcestershire sauce

BASTE

2 tbsp.   melted butter
             Juice of 1 lemon
2 tbsp.   finely chopped fresh dill
             Salt and pepper

Mix all Russian mayonnaise ingredients together and chill until ready to serve.

Combine baste ingredients. Place salmon steaks on well-oiled grill above medium-hot coals. Baste often while fish is cooking. Cook for 5 to 8 minutes on each side, turning carefully with a metal spatula. Serve warm with Russian mayonnaise.

Poultry and Game

Small chickens are best for barbecuing. Cut them in half and cook bone side down first, then turn them over, remembering to baste frequently. Poultry can also be cooked on a rotisserie.

To test whether poultry is cooked, make an incision near the bone. When there are no traces of pink flesh and the juices run absolutely clear, the chicken is ready. Another way to test is to move the drumstick up and down. If it is very flexible, then the meat is cooked. If you have a meat thermometer, use it on poultry, too. Poultry must be cooked through and never served rare.

Game responds very well to marinades, which help to subdue that "gamey" flavor. A marinade is also a good tenderizer.

Ducks cook very well on the barbecue, particularly if they are first washed in honeyed water and then allowed to dry. We recommend the use of a covered barbecue or a rotisserie as ducks require long, slow cooking.

CHAMPAGNE CHICKEN WITH AVOCADO AND LEMON SAUCE

Serves 4

8	chicken drumsticks

MARINADE

½ cup	champagne
2 tbsp.	vegetable oil
	Juice of 1 lemon
1 tsp.	grated lemon zest
1 tbsp.	finely chopped shallots
1 tbsp.	chopped fresh parsley
2 tsp.	fresh thyme
2	bay leaves, crumbled
1	clove garlic, crushed
2 tsp.	peppercorns
	Salt

SAUCE

2	avocados, peeled and stoned
	Juice of 1 lemon
1	clove garlic, crushed
¼ cup	sour cream
	Salt
	Parsley and paprika for garnish

Make deep slits in the drumsticks so the marinade will permeate the meat. Place drumsticks in a flat ceramic or glass dish. Mix marinade ingredients together and pour over chicken. Cover and refrigerate for 12 hours, turning occasionally.

To make sauce, blend avocados, lemon juice, garlic, sour cream and salt. When smooth, spoon into a glass serving bowl and garnish with paprika and parsley.

Remove chicken from marinade, reserving marinade.

Place drumsticks on a barbecue grill over medium-hot coals. Cook 20 to 25 minutes, turning often to prevent burning. Baste frequently with marinade. Serve with sauce.

CHICKEN WITH RED CURRANT AND MUSTARD GLAZE

Serves 8

8	chicken legs (drumsticks and thighs)
	Salt

GLAZE

2 tbsp.	unsalted butter
2	cloves garlic, crushed
1 tbsp.	brown sugar
1 tbsp.	sherry
¼ cup	red currant jelly
1 tbsp.	prepared English mustard
1 tbsp.	Dijon mustard

Wash and pat dry chicken pieces. Rub a little salt into both sides of the chicken. Set aside.

To make sauce, melt butter in a small saucepan. Add garlic. Sauté for about 1 minute. Stir in brown sugar, then add remaining ingredients. Cook 4 to 5 minutes.

Place chicken pieces on an oiled grill over hot coals. Baste frequently with glaze, turning often, for 30 to 35 minutes or until chicken juices run clear.

Just before serving, add a thick coat of glaze. Serve immediately.

TRINIDAD CHICKEN BREASTS

Serves 4

4	whole chicken breasts, cut in half and boned
2 tbsp.	vegetable oil

STUFFING

1 lb.	sweet potatoes, peeled and coarsely chopped
½	onion, finely chopped
2 tsp.	butter
1 tbsp.	brown sugar
2 tsp.	grated orange zest
	Juice of 1 orange
	Juice of ½ lemon
	Salt
	Freshly ground pepper

BASTE

2 tbsp.	melted butter
	Juice of ½ lemon
	Juice of ½ orange
	Pinch nutmeg
½ tsp.	cinnamon

To make stuffing, place sweet potatoes in boiling salted water for 15 to 18 minutes or until tender. Drain and mash. Set aside.

Sauté onion in butter until soft and transparent. Add brown sugar, orange zest, orange and lemon juice, salt and pepper. Add mixture to mashed sweet potato and mix well. Set aside to cool.

Place chicken breasts between two pieces of plastic wrap. Pound to flatten. Spoon a small amount of sweet potato stuffing on each breast. Roll chicken, being careful to tuck in the sides so the stuffing does not spill out. Fasten each breast with a small skewer.

Fry the rolled chicken in hot oil, turning often, until golden brown. Remove from frying pan and take out skewers carefully.

In a small bowl, combine all baste ingredients.

Place rolled chicken on barbecue grill over hot coals and cook 10 to 12 minutes, basting frequently and turning often to prevent burning.

CINNAMON CHICKEN

Serves 4

2½ lbs.   chicken, split in half

MARINADE

⅓ cup	lemon juice
⅓ cup	safflower oil
¼ cup	honey
1	clove garlic, crushed
1 tsp.	cinnamon
1 tsp.	curry powder
¾ tsp.	salt
	Freshly ground black pepper

The day before the barbecue, clean chicken thoroughly. Place chicken in a glass or ceramic dish. Mix marinade ingredients. Pour over chicken halves. Cover and refrigerate overnight, turning chicken occasionally.

Remove chicken from dish, reserving marinade. Bring chicken and marinade back to room temperature.

Grill chicken over medium-hot coals for 30 to 35 minutes, basting with marinade and turning often to prevent burning. Check to see if chicken is cooked by inserting a sharp knife into the flesh near the bone. When juices run clear, chicken is ready. Serve immediately.

TANDOORI-STYLE CHICKEN

Serves 4

2½ lbs.	whole chicken, cut into serving pieces

MARINADE

1	onion, coarsely chopped
2	cloves garlic, minced
1-inch piece	fresh ginger root, peeled and finely chopped
	Juice of ½ lemon
½ tsp.	garam masala
½ tsp.	ground cumin
½ tsp.	ground cardamon
	Pinch chili powder
½ tsp.	turmeric
2 tbsp.	oil
	Salt
1 cup	plain yogurt

The day before the barbecue, make deep slits in the chicken pieces and place them in a large glass or ceramic dish.

Place onion, garlic, ginger, lemon juice, garam masala, cumin, cardamon, chili, turmeric, oil and salt in a blender. Process until well mixed, then stir in yogurt.

Rub onion and yogurt mixture into chicken pieces, working it into the slits. Cover and refrigerate overnight, turning chicken occasionally.

Remove chicken from dish, reserving marinade. Cook on grill over medium-hot coals for 25 to 30 minutes, basting often with marinade and turning frequently. Serve immediately.

POULET DIABLE

Serves 8

8	chicken legs

STUFFING

2	small onions, finely chopped
2 tbsp.	butter
1 cup	breadcrumbs
2 tbsp.	finely chopped fresh parsley
	Dash Worcestershire sauce
1½ tsp.	Dijon mustard
1	egg yolk, beaten
	Salt
	Freshly ground black pepper

To make stuffing: in a saucepan, sauté onions in butter until transparent. Remove from heat. Stir in breadcrumbs. Add remaining stuffing ingredients. Mix well.

Work skin away from flesh of chicken legs. (Do not remove it completely.) Put a small amount of stuffing under the skin of each leg.

Place each leg on a piece of foil, shiny side touching chicken. Seal foil. Place wrapped chicken on a grill over medium-hot coals. Cook 30 minutes or until juices run clear.

Remove chicken from foil and place directly on the grill for a few minutes to crisp the skin. Turn often.

BRAZILIAN CHICKEN

Serves 4

8	half chicken breasts, skinned and boned
2	firm bananas, peeled and cut in half lengthwise

STUFFING

1 cup	butter
1 to 2 tsp.	chili powder
1/2 cup	desiccated coconut
6 drops	hot pepper sauce
	Pinch garlic salt

BASTE

1/4 cup	coconut milk
2 tbsp.	fresh lime juice
1 tsp.	granulated sugar
1 tsp.	grated fresh ginger root
1	clove garlic, crushed
1 tbsp.	olive oil

Place chicken breasts between two pieces of plastic wrap. Pound to flatten. Set aside.

To make stuffing, cream butter with chili powder. Beat in desiccated coconut. Add hot pepper sauce and garlic salt. Mix well.

Spoon a small amount of stuffing on each chicken breast. Roll chicken around stuffing and tuck in the sides. Fasten with a skewer.

Combine all baste ingredients in a bowl. Stir well, then set aside.

Place chicken on barbecue grill at a medium distance above the hot coals. Cook 20 minutes, turning frequently and basting constantly. During the last few minutes of cooking, place bananas on grill. Turn once. Serve 2 chicken pieces with a half a hot banana.

ROCK CORNISH GAME HENS WITH BRANDY

Serves 4

You will need a rotisserie for this recipe.

4	rock Cornish game hens
8	strips bacon
	Freshly ground pepper
	Salt
¼ cup	brandy

Wrap each bird in two strips of bacon and secure with kitchen string or small skewers. Thread the birds on a spit. Place a drip pan under the rotisserie to catch the juices.

Rotate the birds on the spit over hot coals for 20 minutes. Remove bacon and continue cooking for 10 to 20 minutes more.

Cut each bird in half and season lightly. Place on plates.

Place brandy in a small saucepan or metal container. Warm brandy, flame and pour over birds. Serve.

CITRUS-GLAZED DUCK

Serves 6

4 lb.	duck
	Salt
	Freshly ground black pepper

GLAZE

1/4 cup	grapefruit marmalade
1/4 cup	hot water
2 tbsp.	orange juice
2 tbsp.	lemon juice
1/2 tsp.	grated fresh ginger root
1/2 tsp.	grated orange zest
1/2 tsp.	grated lemon zest
1	clove garlic, crushed

Clean duck thoroughly and cut into serving portions. Place pieces in a glass or ceramic dish large enough to hold the pieces lying flat. Prick the skin of the duck all over and season with salt and pepper.

In a saucepan, combine glaze ingredients. Cook, stirring constantly, for several minutes or until marmalade has melted.

Pour glaze over duck and let stand for at least 2 hours.

Remove duck from dish, reserving glaze. Place duck portions on a well-oiled barbecue grill over medium-hot coals. Cook 15 to 20 minutes on each side, basting often with glaze. Don't worry if the skin burns a little.

STUFFED QUAIL

Serves 4 to 8

8	quail
16	grape vine leaves or
8	banana leaves
24	thin strips pork back fat

STUFFING

2 tbsp.	butter
2	onions, finely chopped
2	stalks celery, finely chopped
¼ lb.	mushrooms, finely chopped
	Salt
	Black pepper
1 cup	fresh breadcrumbs
1	egg, beaten
1 tbsp.	cognac

To make stuffing, melt butter in a large frying pan. Add onions and celery and cook, stirring frequently, until vegetables are soft. Add mushrooms and cook for a few minutes, stirring often. Add salt and pepper.

Place breadcrumbs in a large bowl. Add contents of frying pan, including juices, to crumbs. Mix in beaten egg and cognac.

Clean quail thoroughly and pat dry. Fill cavities with stuffing.

Wrap each quail in 2 oiled vine leaves or 1 banana leaf. Cover with 3 strips of pork back fat and wrap in a triple thickness of buttered aluminum foil, or in wet newspaper.

Place wrapped quail on a grill over medium-hot coals. Cook for 35 minutes, turning frequently. Remove foil or newspaper and serve.

VENISON WITH PORT AND CRANBERRIES

Serves 4

| 4 ½-inch | slices venison steak |
| | Salt to taste |

MARINADE

2 tbsp.	whole cranberry sauce
2 tbsp.	port
¼ cup	frozen orange juice concentrate
	Generous pinch cinnamon
	Pinch nutmeg
	Freshly ground black pepper

The day before the barbecue, place venison in a glass or ceramic dish. Mix together marinade ingredients and pour over the venison. Cover and place in the refrigerator for 24 hours, turning steaks occasionally.

Remove venison from marinade. Barbecue steaks over hot coals for 4 to 6 minutes each side, basting often with marinade. Season to taste.

NOTE: Venison should be served rare.

RABBIT WITH SAGE

Serves 6

2 2-lb.	young rabbits, cut into serving pieces

MARINADE

½ cup	olive oil
¼ cup	dry white wine
¼ cup	lemon juice
2 tbsp.	finely chopped fresh sage
4	cloves garlic, crushed
1 tsp.	salt
	Coarsely ground black pepper

Place rabbit pieces in a glass or ceramic dish. Mix together marinade ingredients. Pour marinade over rabbit and refrigerate overnight, turning once.

Remove rabbit pieces and brush with marinade. Place them in a hinged wire basket fairly close to hot coals to sear meat.

Raise grill and cook slowly, basting frequently with marinade and turning often, for about 15 to 20 minutes, or until rabbit is well done.

GUINEA FOWL IN PORT AND PLUM MARINADE

Serves 4

2 2-lb.   medium-sized guinea fowl

MARINADE

½ cup	olive oil
¼ cup	port
¼ cup	raspberry vinegar
2 tbsp.	plum sauce
1 slice	onion
½ tsp.	freshly ground black pepper
½ tsp.	granulated sugar
2	whole cloves

The day before the barbecue, cut tendons at the joints of the guinea fowl. Split the birds in half down the breast bone but leave them in one piece. Remove giblets and clean birds thoroughly. Place birds in a glass or ceramic dish cut-side down. Prick the skin all over.

Mix together marinade ingredients. Pour over birds. Marinate, covered loosely, for at least 12 hours, turning occasionally.

Remove birds from glass dish, reserving marinade. Place birds on well-oiled barbecue grill, bone-side down, over medium-hot coals. Cook 25 to 30 minutes, brushing frequently with marinade.

Turn birds over and cook 25 to 30 minutes more, still brushing with marinade. Birds will be brown and tender when cooked.

ORANGE AND COINTREAU MARINATED PHEASANT

Serves 4

2½ lb.   pheasant

MARINADE

¼ cup	olive oil
¼ cup	white wine
¼ cup	frozen orange juice concentrate
2 tbsp.	Cointreau
	Juice of ½ lemon
	Freshly ground black pepper
	Salt
	Zest of ½ orange

The day before the barbecue, clean pheasant thoroughly and cut into 4 pieces. Place pheasant in a glass or ceramic dish. Mix together marinade ingredients and pour over bird. Make sure all pieces are covered by marinade. Marinate, covered, for 12 to 24 hours, turning occasionally.

Remove pheasant from dish, reserving marinade. Place pheasant pieces on well-oiled barbecue grill. Cook over medium-hot coals 20 to 30 minutes, basting with marinade and turning often to prevent burning.

Just before serving, brush generously with marinade.

ANNIE'S SPECIAL SPICY CHICKEN

Serves 8

If you prefer milder chicken, halve the quantity of the spices.

2 2½-lb.	chickens
¼ cup	sesame seeds

MARINADE

½ cup	catsup
1 tsp.	chili powder
1 tsp.	salt
½ tsp.	cayenne pepper
½ tsp.	ground cumin
½ tsp.	garam masala
	Juice of ½ lemon
2	cloves garlic, crushed

Cut chicken into quarters and remove skin. Lie pieces flat in a baking dish. Mix together marinade ingredients and pour over chicken pieces. Turn pieces so they are well coated. Cover with plastic wrap or foil and chill for 3 to 4 hours.

Remove chicken pieces, reserving marinade. Place chicken pieces bone-side down on a barbecue grill over medium-hot coals. Cook 15 to 20 minutes, or until well browned but not burned.

Turn pieces over and barbecue for another 15 to 20 minutes, basting thoroughly with marinade.

To serve, sprinkle chicken pieces with sesame seeds.

Beef

A great steak should be marbled throughout, with a strong red color and the fat white, not yellow. Beef that is marbled throughout with fat is far more tender than very lean meat.

When barbecuing, follow these guidelines to get the best from your beef:

Rub beef fat on the hot barbecue grill instead of greasing it with butter or oil. This will enhance the flavor of your steaks.

Steaks should be at room temperature before barbecuing.

Always use a spatula or tongs to turn steak. Never poke the meat with a fork or you will release the flavorsome juices.

Never salt your beef while it is cooking. Season after you have finished barbecuing. Salt draws the juices out.

If you are barbecuing a whole filet on a spit, ask your butcher to lard it with strips of salt pork and wrap it with beef suet strips. Use a meat thermometer to make sure the meat is cooked the way you like it.

To prevent the fat on your steaks from curling, cut several small incisions in the gristle.

If you prefer your steak rare, sear it on both sides and cook it quickly. For medium-rare, medium and well-done, sear on both sides for 1 minute close to the hot coals, then raise the grill to finish barbecuing.

Steaks suitable for barbecuing are whole filet, châteaubriand, filet steak (mignon), tournedos, medallions, sirloin or entrecôte, porterhouse, T-bone and rump steak.

Marinades tenderize the meat and enhance flavor. For best results, marinate beef overnight to give the flavor time to permeate the meat.

TAJ MAHAL STEAK

Serves 4

| 4 1-inch | filets mignon |
| | salt |

MARINADE

½ cup	plain yogurt
¼ cup	vegetable oil
	Finely grated zest of 2 limes or lemons
	Juice of 2 limes or lemons
2	cloves garlic, crushed
2 tsp.	ground cumin
1 tsp.	ground cardamon
½ tsp.	cayenne pepper

Place steaks in a shallow glass or ceramic dish. Mix together all marinade ingredients and pour over meat. Leave for 3 to 4 hours, turning occasionally.

Remove steaks from dish, reserving the marinade. Place meat on grill over hot coals and cook for about 6 to 8 minutes on each side (rare to medium-rare). Baste often with the marinade. Add salt to taste.

TOURNEDOS ROSSINI

Serves 4

4 1½-inch	tournedos
	Freshly ground black pepper
2 tbsp.	cognac
¼ lb.	pâté de foie (or high-quality pâté)
	Salt

Season steaks with freshly ground black pepper and grill over hot coals for 7 to 9 minutes on each side (medium-rare).

While meat is cooking, stir cognac into the pâté and mix well.

Just before serving the steaks, spread one side of each with some of the pâté mixture and cook pâté-side up for 30 seconds more. Season to taste.

QUICK STEAK

Serves 4

4	minute steaks
4	cloves garlic, crushed
16 drops	hot pepper sauce
4 tbsp.	German mustard
	Salt

Rub both sides of the steaks with crushed garlic. Sprinkle a couple of drops of hot pepper sauce on both sides of each. Then spread mustard evenly on both sides of each steak.

Barbecue steaks over hot coals 30 seconds on each side (for medium-rare). Season to taste.

FILETS MIGNON IMPERIALES

Serves 4

4 1-inch   filets mignon

SAUCE

2 oz.	blue cheese
1 tbsp.	lemon juice
1½ tbsp.	catsup
1 tsp.	Worcestershire sauce
⅛ lb.	salted cashews, chopped roughly
	Freshly ground black pepper

Mix together the sauce ingredients, making sure the cheese is well blended.

Barbecue steaks for 5 to 8 minutes each side.

Spread sauce on steaks and serve immediately.

WHISKEY FILETS

Serves 2

4 4-oz.	filets mignon
	Salt
	Freshly ground black pepper

MARINADE

2	cloves garlic, crushed
1 tbsp.	grated fresh ginger root
½ cup	soy sauce
2 tbsp.	brown sugar
½ cup	Scotch whiskey
1 tsp.	cornstarch

The day before the barbecue, place filets mignon in a shallow ceramic or glass dish.

Combine marinade ingredients. Pour over meat. Cover with plastic wrap and refrigerate overnight.

The next day, bring meat and marinade back to room temperature. (This will take 3 to 4 hours.) Remove meat from dish and set aside marinade.

Place filets on a well-oiled barbecue grill over hot coals. Cook 5 to 6 minutes on each side for rare; 7 minutes on each side for medium-rare. Brush frequently with marinade. Season to taste.

To make sauce for the beef, reduce the marinade. To thicken, add cornstarch mixed with a few drops of water and cook for about 2 minutes.

KOREAN BEEF

Serves 6

6 1-inch	rib eye steaks
¼ cup	sesame seeds
	Salt

MARINADE

¼ cup	sesame oil
¼ cup	lightly packed brown sugar
¼ cup	soy sauce
2 tbsp.	finely chopped shallots
2	cloves garlic, crushed
1 tbsp.	grated fresh ginger root
	Freshly ground black pepper

The day before the barbecue, place beef in a ceramic or glass dish. Mix marinade ingredients together. Pour over beef. Cover with plastic wrap and refrigerate overnight, turning meat several times.

The next day, bring meat and marinade back to room temperature. (This will take 3 to 4 hours.) Place beef on well-oiled barbecue grill. Sear, then cook for 6 to 8 minutes each side (for rare to medium-rare), basting frequently with marinade. Turn meat only once.

At serving time, sprinkle sesame seeds on each piece of beef and season to taste.

MOROCCAN BEEF

Serves 4

4 1-inch	strip loin steaks
	Salt

MARINADE

1	large Spanish onion, grated
¼ cup	finely chopped parsley
2 tbsp.	sour cream
1 tsp.	ground cumin seeds
½ tsp.	cayenne pepper
½ tsp.	garam masala
	Freshly ground black pepper

Trim excess fat from meat and place meat in a shallow glass or ceramic dish. Combine marinade ingredients. Spread marinade thickly over both sides of the steaks. Cover and leave for 2 to 3 hours.

Barbecue steaks over hot coals for 5 to 8 minutes on each side (for rare to medium-rare). Season to taste.

NOTE: There is no need to scrape off the marinade before barbecuing, as it adds to the flavor of the beef.

STEAK AU POIVRE VERT

Serves 4

1½ lbs.	sirloin steak
¼ cup	drained green peppercorns, crushed
	Salt

MARINADE

½ cup	red wine vinegar
⅓ cup	vegetable or olive oil
	Few drops hot pepper sauce
1 tsp.	chopped fresh marjoram
1 tsp.	chopped fresh thyme
2	bay leaves, crumbled
1	large onion, coarsely chopped
2	cloves garlic, crushed

The day before the barbecue, trim excess fat from meat. Place steaks in a shallow ceramic or glass dish. Mix together marinade ingredients and pour over steaks. Cover dish and marinate steaks overnight, turning steaks occasionally.

The next day, remove steaks from marinade. Press crushed peppercorns into both sides of the steaks.

Grill over hot coals for 6 to 9 minutes each side (for rare to medium-rare). Turn once only. Season to taste.

ENTRECÔTES WITH BERCY BUTTER

Serves 4

4 1-inch	entrecôte steaks
	Freshly ground black pepper
	Salt

BERCY BUTTER

1 cup	dry white wine
1 tbsp.	finely chopped shallots
½ cup	unsalted butter, at room temperature
½ lb.	bone marrow (available on request from the butcher) poached in salted water and finely chopped
	Juice of ½ lemon
1	clove garlic, crushed
¼ cup	chopped fresh parsley
5 drops	hot pepper sauce
	Salt
	Freshly ground black pepper

To make butter, in a saucepan, combine white wine and shallots. Bring to a boil. Turn down heat and simmer until liquid is reduced by half. Allow to cool completely.

When wine is cool, blend in softened butter a little at a time with an electric beater. Add bone marrow, lemon juice, garlic, chopped parsley, hot pepper sauce, salt and pepper and beat well. Set aside.

Trim excess fat off steaks. Season steaks generously with black pepper. Place on a well-oiled grill over hot coals. Cook 5 minutes on each side (for rare to medium-rare). Season to taste.

Serve each steak topped with a spoonful of Bercy butter.

FILETS MIGNON MIRABEAU

Serves 4

4 1-inch	filet mignon steaks
8	stuffed green olives, sliced, for garnish

ANCHOVY BUTTER

2 2-oz. cans anchovies	
½ cup	softened unsalted butter
1	clove garlic, crushed
1 tsp.	cognac
	Freshly ground black pepper

Drain the anchovies and place them in cold water. Soak for 10 minutes, then drain again. Pat dry with paper towels. Place anchovies, butter, garlic, cognac and pepper in a blender. Process until smooth. Place in a small bowl and refrigerate until ready to use.

Barbecue steaks on a well-oiled grill over hot coals for 5 minutes each side (for medium-rare). Season to taste.

To serve, dot with anchovy butter and garnish with sliced olives.

CHÂTEAUBRIAND WITH MAÎTRE D'HÔTEL BUTTER

Serves 2

1 2-inch	châteaubriand filet
½ lb.	bone marrow
	(available on request from the butcher)
1 tbsp.	butter
	Pinch salt
	Pinch cayenne pepper
2	shallots, peeled but left whole

MAÎTRE D'HÔTEL BUTTER

¼ cup	unsalted butter, softened
1 tbsp.	finely chopped fresh parsley
2 tsp.	chopped fresh chives
	Salt
	Pinch freshly ground black pepper
1 tbsp.	Dijon mustard
1 tbsp.	lemon juice

To make the maître d'hôtel butter: in a small bowl, beat the butter with a wooden spoon. Gently work in the remaining butter ingredients. When well blended, place on waxed paper or aluminum foil. Roll into a cylinder. Twist both ends to seal and set aside.

With a narrow knife, make a tunnel-like incision through the middle of the châteaubriand, almost to the end.

In a small frying pan, lightly brown the bone marrow in butter. Season with salt and cayenne pepper. Stuff the châteaubriand with the whole shallots and the bone marrow.

Barbecue steak over hot coals for about 5 minutes on each side to seal in the juices.

Cook for a further 10 minutes each side (for a large filet). To serve, top steaks with slices of maître d'hôtel butter.

PORTERHOUSE STEAKS WITH BÉARNAISE SAUCE

Serves 4

4 1-inch	porterhouse steaks
	Freshly ground black pepper
	Salt

BÉARNAISE SAUCE

¼ cup	tarragon white wine vinegar
¼ cup	dry white wine
1 tbsp.	finely chopped onion
1½ tbsp.	chopped fresh tarragon, crushed
2 tsp.	chopped fresh chervil, crushed (optional)
	Salt
	Freshly ground black pepper
	Pinch ground thyme
	Pinch crumbled bay leaf
4	egg yolks
2 tsp.	water
1 cup	softened butter
	Pinch cayenne pepper
	Squeeze lemon juice

In the top of a double boiler, combine vinegar and wine. Place over direct heat. Add onion, most of the tarragon and chervil, salt, pepper, thyme and bay leaf. Reduce until liquid measures about 2 tbsp. Remove from heat and cool.

Place top of double boiler over simmering water. (Do not let the water touch the bottom of the top of the double boiler.) Stir together egg yolks and water and add to saucepan. Beat with a wire whisk. Do not allow to boil or the eggs will curdle. As soon as the mixture becomes light and fluffy add the butter a little piece at a time. Continue to whisk.

When mixture is smooth and has the consistency of mayonnaise, strain it. Just before serving, add the remaining tarragon and chervil. Season with cayenne pepper and lemon juice. Keep warm.

Season steaks with pepper. Place them on a well-oiled grill over hot coals. Cook 6 minutes (rare) to 9 minutes (medium-rare) on each side. Season. Serve with warm béarnaise sauce.

SIRLOIN STEAKS WITH HORSERADISH BUTTER

Serves 4

| 4 1-inch | sirloin steaks |
| | Salt |

HORSERADISH BUTTER

2 tbsp.	unsalted butter, softened
2	shallots, peeled and finely chopped
1½ tbsp.	prepared horseradish
1 tbsp.	white vinegar
	Freshly ground black pepper

To make horseradish butter, whip butter until smooth. Add shallots, horseradish, vinegar and pepper. Mix well and place in a butter dish or small bowl. Cover and refrigerate until ready to use.

Trim excess fat from steaks, then sprinkle steaks with pepper. Place on well-oiled barbecue grill over hot coals. Cook 5 minutes (rare) to 7 minutes (medium-rare) on each side.

Serve each steak with a pat of horseradish butter and a little salt.

Lamb

Lamb is served pink or well done. If you follow our recipes, your lamb will be pink in the middle and brown on the outside.

Lamb cuts suitable for barbecuing are boned rolled shoulder, loin chops, rib chops, cutlets (boneless slices cut from a leg of lamb), shoulder chops, rack of lamb and leg of lamb.

Before barbecuing, bring your meat back to room temperature if it has been refrigerated.

Seasoning lamb with fresh herbs such as rosemary or mint can be delicious and flavorsome.

Always cook lamb uncovered to obtain the best flavor from the meat.

Don't forget to oil your grill before cooking.

Never use a fork to turn lamb. You will lose valuable meat juices. We suggest a spatula or tongs.

Salt your lamb *after* cooking, so it doesn't dry out and lose its moistness.

LAMB AU VIN ROUGE

Serves 6

12 1-inch	loin chops
	Salt

MARINADE

½ cup	Burgundy
¼ cup	olive oil
6	black peppercorns, crushed
2	cloves garlic, crushed
1 tsp.	cumin seeds, crushed
1	medium onion, coarsely chopped

The day before the barbecue, put the chops in a shallow ceramic or glass dish so that they lie flat. You may need two dishes.

Combine marinade ingredients in a screw-top jar. Shake well to blend. Pour over chops. Cover chops with plastic wrap and refrigerate overnight.

Bring chops and marinade back to room temperature. Drain, reserving marinade.

Place chops on a grill over medium-hot coals. Cook 12 to 14 minutes, brushing often with marinade and turning chops frequently. Season to taste.

CALIFORNIAN LAMB CHOPS

Serves 8

16 1-inch	lamb rib chops
	Salt

STUFFING

1 tbsp.	butter
1	large onion, finely chopped
2	cloves garlic, finely chopped
1 cup	fresh white breadcrumbs
¼ cup	raisins
2 tbsp.	currants
	Grated zest of 2 oranges
2 tbsp.	chopped fresh mint
½ tsp.	dried thyme
1 tsp.	finely chopped fresh parsley
	Salt
	Freshly ground black pepper
	Juice of 1 orange

GLAZE

2 tbsp.	brown sugar
	Juice of ½ lemon
	Juice of 1 orange
2 tbsp.	grapefruit or orange marmalade
	Few drops Worcestershire sauce

To make stuffing, fry onion and garlic in butter until transparent. Place in a bowl and add remaining stuffing ingredients except orange juice. Mix, then add orange juice. Stir.

Cut a pocket in each lamb chop. Pack stuffing into the cavities. Fasten chops with skewers.

Place glaze ingredients in a small saucepan and cook over a low heat for 1 to 2 minutes, stirring with a wooden spoon.

Place chops on a well-oiled grill above an even bed of glowing coals. Cook 6 minutes each side, constantly basting with glaze. Make sure stuffing does not fall out. Season and serve.

LAMB CUTLETS WITH HONEY CHUTNEY BASTE

Serves 4

8	lamb cutlets
	Freshly ground black pepper
	Salt

HONEY-CHUTNEY BASTE

2	medium onions, finely chopped
2	cloves garlic, finely chopped
2 tbsp.	vegetable oil
^{1}/$_3$ cup	hot Bengal chutney
^{1}/$_4$ cup	liquid honey
1 tsp.	curry powder
1 tbsp.	fresh lemon juice

Season lamb cutlets with pepper.

In a heavy saucepan over moderate heat, fry onions and garlic in oil until golden. Add remaining baste ingredients. Cook, stirring with a wooden spoon, for about 3 minutes.

Grill cutlets over medium-hot coals for 3 to 4 minutes each side, or until browned. Brush cutlets with baste and cook for another 2 minutes on each side. Heat remaining sauce. Season lamb and serve with hot sauce.

MARINATED FRUIT LAMB CHOPS

Serves 4

8 1-inch	lamb loin chops
	Salt

MARINADE

1 lb.	dried apricots
½ lb.	prunes, pitted
2 cups	orange juice
1 cup	lemon juice
¾ cup	firmly packed brown sugar
½ tsp.	ground allspice
½ tsp.	ground cinnamon
½ tsp.	ground cloves
	Pinch nutmeg
¼ cup	vegetable oil

The night before the barbecue, place apricots and prunes in water. Soak overnight.

In the morning, drain apricots and prunes and place in a blender or food processor. Add orange juice, lemon juice, brown sugar, allspice, cinnamon, cloves and nutmeg. Process until puréed.

Place lamb chops in a glass dish. Cover with fruit purée and marinate for at least 12 hours.

Remove lamb from glass dish. Pour marinade into a saucepan. Add oil and bring to the boil. Simmer for 10 minutes.

Place meat on grill over medium-hot coals and cook thoroughly until browned, basting frequently with marinade and turning often. Season to taste. Serve any remaining marinade with chops.

TARRAGON LAMB CHOPS

Serves 4

8 ¾-inch	lamb loin chops
	Salt
	Freshly ground black pepper

MARINADE

¼ cup	vegetable oil
2	cloves garlic, crushed
¼ cup	dry white wine
2 tbsp.	tomato paste
2 tbsp.	tarragon vinegar
1 tsp.	dry mustard
4 to 5 sprigs	fresh tarragon

Place chops flat in a shallow ceramic or glass dish. Combine marinade ingredients, then pour over chops. Cover with plastic wrap and refrigerate for at least 2 hours, turning chops occasionally.

Drain chops, reserving marinade. Bring chops and marinade back to room temperature.

Place chops on a grill over medium-hot coals. Brush generously with marinade and cook for 6 to 7 minutes on each side, basting often. Season and serve.

WEST INDIAN LAMB

Serves 4

| 4 to 6 | lamb rib chops |
| | Salt |

MARINADE

¼ cup	olive oil
¼ cup	lemon juice
2 tbsp.	finely chopped fresh coriander
1 tbsp.	curry powder
½ tsp.	turmeric
½ tsp.	cayenne pepper
¼ tsp.	powdered ginger

Place chops in a shallow ceramic or glass dish. Mix marinade ingredients well and spread over lamb. Cover with plastic wrap and place in the refrigerator for at least 2 hours, turning meat several times. Remove from marinade and bring back to room temperature. (Discard marinade.)

Place chops on an oiled grill close to medium-hot coals and barbecue for about 6 minutes on each side. Season to taste.

INDIAN LEG OF LAMB

Serves 6

5 lbs.	leg of lamb, boned, trimmed and rolled

PASTE

1	medium onion, grated
2 to 3	cloves garlic
2 tbsp.	finely chopped fresh ginger root
2 tsp.	ground cumin
2 tsp.	ground coriander
1½ tsp.	salt
1 tsp.	turmeric
½ tsp.	chili powder or sambal oelek
½ tsp.	ground cinnamon
½ tsp.	ground cardamon
	Juice of 1 lemon

PURÉE

¼ lb.	blanched almonds and/or cashews
1 cup	natural yogurt

Start at least two days before the barbecue. Make deep incisions into the fleshy parts of the lamb. Combine paste ingredients. Rub paste into the slits and place a little in the cavity where the bone has been removed.

To make purée, place the nuts and yogurt in food processor or blender and blend until puréed. Spoon purée over the paste. Marinate lamb for 36 to 48 hours in the refrigerator.

Bring lamb back to room temperature. Wrap lamb in a double thickness of aluminum foil and seal. Cook for 1 hour to 1 hour and 30 minutes on a barbecue grill over medium-hot coals, or until cooked to desired doneness, turning occasionally.

Remove lamb from foil. Place directly on the grill and barbecue until nicely browned. Let rest for 5 minutes, then carve. Serve with hot spiced rice.

GINGER-GLAZED LAMB

Serves 4

8   lamb loin chops
           Salt
           Freshly ground black pepper

GLAZE

2 tbsp.   ginger marmalade
2 tbsp.   vegetable oil
1 tbsp.   lemon juice
1 tsp.   grated fresh ginger root

Season chops with salt and pepper. In a small saucepan, heat marmalade, oil, lemon juice and freshly grated ginger.

Brush chops with glaze and place on an oiled grill over medium-hot coals. Barbecue for 6 to 7 minutes on each side, or until cooked to desired doneness, basting frequently with glaze.

SPANISH LAMB

Serves 6 to 8

1	leg of lamb, boned
¼ cup	hot bacon fat
⅓ cup	water
½ tsp.	cornstarch
	Salt

MARINADE

1½ cups	port
1 cup	water
1 tbsp.	chopped fresh basil
1 tbsp.	chopped fresh oregano
1 tbsp.	chopped fresh rosemary
¼ cup	whole peppercorns

Trim any excess fat from lamb and place lamb in a ceramic or glass dish.

In a saucepan, combine all marinade ingredients. Bring to a boil, then simmer for 10 minutes. Pour over lamb. Let stand for 24 hours, basting and turning frequently.

Drain lamb, reserving marinade. Heat the marinade and pour in bacon drippings. Stir until well blended.

Secure lamb on a spit over hot coals. Turn often, basting with marinade. The lamb should take about 1 hour and 30 minutes if you like it pink, 2 hours if you like it well done.

To make gravy, strain remaining marinade. Add the water and cook over moderate heat. Add cornstarch mixed with a few drops of water, stirring constantly with a wooden spoon until thickened. Season to taste. Serve lamb with gravy.

Pork

Choose lean pork. Trim off any excess fat because it will spit and cause smoke and flames.

Pork needs to be cooked over an even, gentle heat rather than over a high heat that sears the meat quickly.

It is no longer considered necessary to cook pork all the way through. However, the decision is yours.

Be sure to oil the barbecue grill with any excess fat you have cut off your meat. This prevents the food from sticking and adds to the flavor of the pork.

Remember to marinate your meat in a glass or ceramic dish; allow enough time for the flavors to penetrate.

Baste and turn pork often so it remains moist and flavorful.

MALAGA PORK CHOPS

Serves 8

8 1½-inch	pork chops
⅓ cup	melted butter
	Salt
	Freshly ground black pepper

STUFFING

2 tbsp.	seedless raisins, chopped
1 tbsp.	dark rum
2 tbsp.	butter
1	cooking apple, peeled, cored and finely chopped
1 tbsp.	finely chopped onion
1 tbsp.	finely chopped celery
¼ cup	chicken stock
1 tbsp.	brown sugar
½ tsp.	salt
	Freshly ground black pepper
1 cup	fresh white breadcrumbs

The day before the barbecue, place raisins and rum in a bowl. Let stand overnight.

The next day, melt butter in a frying pan over moderate heat. Add apple and cook 2 minutes, or until soft. Add onion, celery, stock, brown sugar, salt and pepper.

Place breadcrumbs in a bowl. Add raisins and any remaining rum. Pour in contents of frying pan and mix thoroughly.

Cut a pocket in the side of each pork chop. Divide stuffing evenly among chops. Fill pockets and secure with toothpicks.

Barbecue chops over medium-hot coals for approximately 10 minutes on each side, basting often with melted butter. Remove toothpicks. Season to taste and serve.

MARINATED PORK CHOPS WITH SAUCE ROBERT

Serves 4

8 1-inch	pork center loin chops
	Salt
	Freshly ground black pepper

MARINADE

1/3 cup	dry white wine
1/3 cup	cognac
2 tbsp.	vegetable oil
2 tsp.	white vinegar
	Freshly ground black pepper

SAUCE ROBERT

2 tbsp.	butter
1	medium onion, grated
2 tsp.	flour
1/2 cup	dry white wine
1/2 cup	beef stock
1 1/2 tsp.	Dijon mustard
	Pinch granulated sugar

The day before the barbecue, place pork chops in a shallow glass or ceramic dish. Season with salt and pepper. Mix marinade ingredients and pour over chops. Cover with plastic wrap and refrigerate overnight.

The next day, remove chops from marinade and bring chops and marinade back to room temperature. Then prepare sauce. In a saucepan, melt butter over low heat. Add onion and cook until transparent. Stir in flour and cook 2 to 3 minutes. Add wine and cook a further 1 minute. Add beef stock and cook for 5 to 8 minutes over very low heat. Remove saucepan from heat and add the mustard and sugar. Stir well. Keep warm, but do not allow sauce to boil after mustard has been added. Place chops over medium-hot coals. Cook about 8 to 10 minutes each side, basting with reserved marinade. Serve with sauce.

PORK CHOPS WITH APRICOT GLAZE

Serves 6

6 1-inch	pork center loin chops
	Salt
	Freshly ground pepper

APRICOT GLAZE

1 tbsp.	butter
1 tbsp.	safflower oil
1	onion, finely chopped
¼ cup	apricot nectar
¼ cup	orange marmalade
¼ cup	apricot jam
2 tbsp.	brown sugar
½ tsp.	ground allspice
	Pinch ground ginger

Season pork chops with salt and pepper on both sides. Set aside.

Heat the butter and oil in a frying pan. Add the onion and cook over low heat until onion is transparent. Add the rest of the glaze ingredients and cook over low heat until well blended and fairly liquid.

Place pork chops on a grill over medium-hot coals. Cook 8 to 10 minutes each side, basting frequently with glaze.

PORC À L'ORANGE

Serves 4

8 ½-inch	pork center loin chops
	Salt
	Freshly ground black pepper

MARINADE

½ cup	frozen concentrated orange juice
2 tbsp.	lemon juice
1 tbsp.	Grand Marnier liqueur
1½ tsp.	brown sugar

The day before the barbecue, place pork chops in a shallow ceramic or glass dish. Combine marinade ingredients in a bowl. Mix well. Pour marinade over chops and marinate overnight, turning occasionally.

The next day, remove chops from dish. Reserve marinade.

Place pork chops over medium-hot coals. Cook 6 to 8 minutes each side, brushing with the marinade and turning often. At the last minute, baste chops generously. Season to taste and serve.

HAM STEAKS WITH ARTICHOKE PURÉE

Serves 4

4 ½-inch	ham steaks
1/4 cup	unsalted butter, melted

ARTICHOKE PURÉE

8	canned artichoke hearts
	Juice of ½ lemon
¼ cup	creamy mashed potatoes
1 tbsp.	Pistachio Butter (page 27) or
1 tbsp.	finely chopped pistachio nuts
	Pinch salt
	Freshly ground black pepper
	Pinch nutmeg

To make the purée, place artichoke hearts, lemon juice, mashed potatoes, pistachio butter, salt, black pepper and nutmeg in a blender or food processor. Process until puréed. Transfer to a small saucepan and place over low heat while ham is cooking.

Brush the ham with melted butter and grill over medium-hot coals until heated and cooked through. About 2 to 3 minutes each side should be sufficient. Serve ham with warm artichoke purée.

PEKING PORK ROLLS

Makes 18 to 24 bite-sized rolls

These rolls can be used as an appetizer or a main course.

½ lb.	pork tenderloin
¼ cup	Hoisin sauce (available in Oriental grocery stores)
18-24	shallots, trimmed and peeled
24	toothpicks, soaked in water for 1 hour
	Chopped fresh coriander for garnish

MARINADE

⅓ cup	soy sauce
2 tbsp.	sherry
2	cloves garlic, sliced
1 tbsp.	brown sugar
2 tsp.	sesame oil
	Freshly ground black pepper

Trim all fat off tenderloin and cut meat lengthwise into 18 to 24 wafer-thin slices. Place pork slices in a shallow ceramic or glass dish. Mix marinade ingredients. Pour over pork slices and marinate at room temperature for 1 hour.

Remove pork from marinade. Discard marinade. Pat pork slices dry. Brush each slice with Hoisin sauce and place 1 shallot in the center of each slice. Roll pork around shallot and skewer with a toothpick.

Place skewered rolls on barbecue grill over medium-hot coals. Cook 20 to 25 minutes, turning often, until evenly browned. Garnish with chopped coriander.

PEANUT PORK TENDERLOIN

Serves 6

6 1-inch	slices pork tenderloin

MARINADE

1	medium onion, coarsely chopped
½ cup	fresh lime or lemon juice
¼ cup	peanut oil
¼ cup	soy sauce
¼ cup	dark rum
2 tbsp.	brown sugar
1 tbsp.	grated fresh ginger root
2	cloves garlic, crushed
¼ cup	smooth peanut butter
½ cup	coconut cream

The day before the barbecue, place pork slices in a shallow ceramic or glass dish.

In a bowl, combine onion, lime juice, peanut oil, soy sauce, rum, brown sugar, ginger and garlic. Mix well. Pour over pork. Cover with plastic wrap and refrigerate overnight, turning meat occasionally. Drain meat, reserving marinade, and bring back to room temperature.

In a small saucepan, bring one quarter of the marinade to the boil. Lower heat and stir in peanut butter. Cook, stirring, over low heat until well mixed. Remove from heat and stir in coconut cream. Keep warm but do not boil.

Barbecue marinated pork slices over medium-hot coals for 8 to 10 minutes on each side, basting with remaining reserved marinade. Transfer meat to a heated platter and pour peanut sauce over it.

GLAZED HAM WITH HONEYDEW MELON

Serves 4

4 1-inch	cooked ham steaks
1	large honeydew melon, peeled and cut into 8 wedges

GLAZE

½ cup	butter
½ cup	fruit chutney
1 tbsp.	curry powder
2 tsp.	prepared English mustard
	Pinch ground ginger

To make glaze, melt butter in a small saucepan over moderate heat. Do not brown. Remove pan from heat and add chutney, curry powder, mustard and ginger. Stir with a wooden spoon.

Place ham in a pan of hot water for 5 minutes to remove some of the salt. Drain.

Place ham steaks and melon slices on a well-oiled barbecue grill over an even layer of medium-hot coals. Brush ham and melon with some of the glaze. Cook ham and melon for 2 to 3 minutes, turning with barbecue tongs or a flat metal spatula. Keep brushing the ham with glaze. Serve each ham slice with 2 wedges of glazed melon.

PIQUANT RASPBERRY PORK CHOPS

Serves 4

4 1-inch	pork center loin chops
	Salt
	Pepper

MARINADE

¼ cup	raspberry jam
¼ cup	boiling water
2 tbsp.	raspberry vinegar
1 tsp.	prepared English mustard
2 tsp.	cinnamon
1 tsp.	lemon juice
	Pinch ground ginger
	Pinch ground cloves

The day before the barbecue, put raspberry jam in a small ovenproof bowl. Add boiling water and stir until well blended. Add the rest of the marinade ingredients and mix.

Place pork chops in a shallow glass or ceramic dish. Pour marinade over chops, coating them well. Cover with plastic wrap and refrigerate overnight, turning meat once.

Drain chops thoroughly, reserving marinade. Place chops above medium-hot coals on a well-oiled grill. Cook 8 to 10 minutes on each side, basting frequently with marinade.

Skewered Food

There are many different names for skewered food. These include kebabs, kabobs, shashliks, shish kebabs and brochettes. They all describe a method of cooking meat, poultry, fish, vegetables or fruit by threading the ingredients on skewers and grilling.

There are several different types of skewers available: metal skewers with or without clamps at each end and wooden or bamboo sticks. You can also use green branches from saplings, stripped of bark and whittled down.

If you decide to use bamboo sticks, remember to soak them for at least an hour before threading them with food and placing them on the barbecue; otherwise they may burn.

Meat for skewer cooking tastes best when marinated in a cool place for at least an hour, overnight if possible.

Don't push your ingredients too closely together on the skewer or they won't cook properly.

One of the main advantages to skewered food is the variety of combinations available. Make up your own and use one of the marinade recipes shown here. After the food has marinated, reserve the liquids and use them to baste the skewers while barbecuing. Skewered food requires lots of basting to bring out the full flavor of the ingredients.

SOUTH AFRICAN SOSATIES

Serves 8

1½ tbsp.	vegetable oil
3	medium onions, finely chopped
1 tsp.	hot curry powder
½ tsp.	ground coriander
1 tsp.	ground cumin
	Pinch turmeric
¼ cup	lime juice
2 tbsp.	apricot jam
2	cloves garlic, crushed
1 tsp.	sambal oelek
2 lbs.	boneless lamb, cut into cubes
½ tsp.	salt
	Freshly ground black pepper
8	metal skewers
12	cocktail onions, peeled

The day before the barbecue, in a large casserole, heat the oil. Gently sauté onions until they are soft and transparent. Add curry powder, coriander, cumin and turmeric. Cook, stirring, for 2 to 3 minutes. Add lime juice to casserole; and apricot jam. Continue cooking until mixture reaches boiling point. Reduce heat and simmer for 15 minutes. Remove from heat and cool. Add garlic and sambal oelek.

Season the lamb cubes with salt and pepper. Add lamb to the curry mixture. Marinate overnight, turning meat occasionally.

Drain lamb and reserve marinade. Thread the meat on the skewers, alternating with onions. Grill 8 to 15 minutes, turning often and brushing with marinade.

VEAL KEBABS WITH KIDNEYS

Serves 8

½ lb.	veal kidneys
	Cold water
4 lbs.	boneless veal, cut in cubes
1 tsp.	salt
	Freshly ground black pepper
1 tsp.	mild paprika
16	cherry tomatoes
16	mushroom caps
2	small onions, chopped into chunks
12	bamboo sticks, soaked in water for 1 hour
6	fresh rosemary sprigs

BASTE

½ cup	melted butter
¼ cup	dry white wine
2	sprigs rosemary, chopped

Soak veal kidneys in cold water for 3 minutes. Trim, skin and core kidneys, then cut them in quarters. Place kidneys and veal in a large bowl. Season with salt, pepper and paprika. Let sit for at least 1 hour.

Combine baste ingredients. Thread the veal, kidneys, tomatoes, mushroom caps and onion alternately on soaked bamboo sticks. Brush with baste.

Toss 4 rosemary sprigs directly on hot coals. Grill kebabs for 10 minutes, turning often and brushing with baste. Chop remaining 2 sprigs of rosemary and sprinkle over the kebabs at the last minute. Turn once and serve.

TAHITIAN PRAWNS

Serves 4

1½ lbs.	raw prawns or large shrimp
½ cup	coconut milk
3 tbsp.	lime juice
1 tbsp.	soy sauce
1 tsp.	granulated sugar
	Grated zest of 1 lime
2	cloves garlic, crushed
1 tsp.	grated fresh ginger root
8	bamboo sticks, soaked in water for 1 hour

Shell prawns or shrimp and remove spinal vein.

Place coconut milk, lime juice, soy sauce, sugar, zest, garlic and ginger in a bowl. Stir. Add prawns and marinate, covered, for 2 hours in the refrigerator.

Bring prawns back to room temperature. Drain, reserving marinade.

Thread 3 or 4 prawns on each bamboo stick. Barbecue over hot coals for about 5 minutes, turning and brushing often with marinade. Just before serving, brush prawns with remaining marinade.

CHICKEN SATAY

Serves 6

1½ lbs.	boned, skinned chicken breasts
12	bamboo sticks, soaked in water for 1 hour
2 tbsp.	peanut oil
	Sprinkling of sesame seeds

MARINADE

2	small fresh red chilies, or
¼ tsp.	sambal oelek, crushed
2	cloves garlic, crushed
¼ cup	soy sauce
2 tbsp.	brown sugar
2 tbsp.	water
2 tbsp.	peanut oil

SATAY SAUCE

½ lb.	fresh roasted peanuts, crushed
3	red chilies, or
½ tsp.	sambal oelek
1	medium-size onion, chopped
2	cloves garlic, finely chopped
½ tsp.	grated fresh ginger root
½ tsp.	dried shrimp paste (available at Oriental grocery stores), dry-fried
1¾ cups	coconut milk
2 tsp.	sugar
	Fresh lime or lemon juice
	Salt

The day before the barbecue, slice chicken into thin strips.

To make marinade, pound chilies and garlic together in a mortar with a pestle. Transfer to a medium-sized bowl. Add soy sauce, brown sugar and water. Drizzle the oil into the bowl a little at a time, stirring constantly. Add chicken pieces. Cover with plastic wrap and marinate chicken overnight.

The next day, drain chicken and bring back to room temperature. While chicken is warming, make the sauce. Put the peanuts, chilies, onion, garlic, ginger and shrimp paste in a blender. Process until mixture forms a paste.

Heat the coconut milk to boiling. Stir in peanut paste and sugar. Cook, stirring constantly, until thickened. Stir in lime juice and salt. Set aside.

Thread 3 or 4 chicken strips on each stick, leaving at least half the stick free at the blunt end. Cook above medium-hot coals for 6 to 8 minutes, turning frequently. Chicken should be crisp and brown.

Remove chicken from heat and brush with peanut oil. Sprinkle with sesame seeds and return to barbecue for 1 to 2 minutes. Serve with satay sauce.

AUSSIE BEEF KEBABS

Serves 4

1½ lbs.	boneless beef, cut in cubes
8	bamboo sticks, soaked in water for 1 hour

MARINADE

¼ cup	catsup
2 tbsp.	Worcestershire sauce
2 tbsp.	vegetable oil
2 tbsp.	onion, chopped
2	cloves garlic, crushed
1 tbsp.	freshly chopped parsley

Place beef in a glass or ceramic dish. Mix marinade ingredients together. Pour marinade over beef. Marinate for 3 to 4 hours, turning occasionally.

Thread beef on bamboo sticks. Barbecue over hot coals for 5 to 6 minutes, turning often.

MIDDLE EASTERN KEBABS

Serves 4

2 lbs.	ground lamb
2	onions, grated
½ cup	finely chopped fresh coriander
½ cup	finely chopped fresh parsley
	Fresh mint, finely chopped
	Juice of 1 lemon
2 tsp.	cinnamon
2 tsp.	cumin
	Pinch cayenne pepper
	Salt
	Pinch nutmeg
1	egg
1 cup	breadcrumbs
4	metal skewers

In a large bowl, combine lamb, onions, coriander, parsley, mint, lemon juice, cinnamon, cumin, cayenne pepper, salt, nutmeg, egg and breadcrumbs. With your hands, mix together into a paste.

Wet your hands and pat meat paste firmly around skewers in a sausage shape.

Cook over hot coals 5 to 8 minutes, being careful not to overcook.

LAMB AND ZUCCHINI SHASHLIK WITH LEMON AND TARRAGON

Serves 4

1½ lbs.	boneless lamb shoulder, trimmed and cut in cubes
4	medium-sized zucchini, thickly sliced
4	metal skewers
	Salt
	Freshly ground black pepper

MARINADE

1 cup	vegetable oil
⅓ cup	lemon juice
4	shallots, chopped
2 tbsp.	chopped fresh tarragon
2 tsp.	tarragon mustard or Dijon mustard

The day before the barbecue, in a large bowl, combine oil, lemon juice, shallots, tarragon and mustard. Toss lamb and zucchini into the marinade. Cover and chill overnight, stirring occasionally.

Drain lamb and zucchini and bring back to room temperature, reserving marinade. Thread lamb alternately with zucchini on metal skewers.

Barbecue kebabs over glowing coals for 12 to 15 minutes. Baste constantly with marinade. Season to taste.

GOURMET SURF AND TURF BROCHETTES

Serves 4

½ lb.	beef rump or strip loin, cut in small cubes
4	raw lobster tails with the flesh removed and cut into chunks, or
1 lb.	raw shrimp, shelled, deveined and cut in halves
8	metal skewers Juice of 1 lime or lemon

BASTE

¼ cup	butter, melted
2	cloves garlic, crushed
1 tbsp.	chopped fresh parsley Salt Freshly ground black pepper

Thread the beef and lobster or shrimp alternately on skewers. Squeeze lime juice over meat and leave for 15 minutes.

To prepare baste, melt the butter and add the rest of the baste ingredients. Heat gently for 2 or 3 minutes.

Grill brochettes over very hot coals for 4 to 5 minutes, turning often and brushing with hot baste.

ISLANDER STICKS

Serves 6

2 lbs.	boneless pork, cut in strips
12	metal skewers
2	firm bananas, peeled and sliced thickly
½ cup	desiccated coconut
	Juice of 1 lime

MARINADE

1 cup	soy sauce
½ cup	firmly packed brown sugar
2	cloves garlic, crushed
1 tbsp.	grated fresh ginger root
¼ cup	medium dry sherry
¼ cup	cold water

Lay pork strips in a single layer in a shallow ceramic or glass dish. Mix marinade ingredients together and pour over the pork. Cover and marinate for at least 30 minutes, turning meat once.

Drain pork, reserving marinade. Weave meat strips on metal skewers, allowing space at the end of each skewer for banana pieces.

Dip banana slices in reserved marinade. Roll in desiccated coconut and sprinkle with lime juice.

Place 1 or 2 banana slices on the end of each skewer. Brush skewered ingredients with more marinade.

Grill for about 10 to 15 minutes over medium-hot coals, or until meat is cooked through.

BANANA AND SCALLOP KEBABS

Serves 6

36	fresh scallops
4 tbsp.	lemon juice
1 tsp.	salt
	Freshly ground black pepper
4	bananas, peeled and sliced
6	slices lean bacon
6	long wooden skewers, soaked in water for 1 hour
¼ cup	butter, melted
1	lemon, cut into six wedges

Rinse scallops in cold water. Spread on paper towels and pat dry.

Combine one half of the lemon juice and the salt and pepper in a glass or ceramic bowl. Add scallops a few at a time, making sure they are well coated. Brush remaining lemon juice onto banana pieces.

Thread scallops, banana slices and bacon on the skewers. Loop the bacon slices up and down to weave over and under the scallops and banana slices. Push scallops and bananas tightly together on the skewer. Brush with melted butter.

Place skewers over medium-hot coals. Cook 4 to 6 minutes, turning frequently and basting often with butter. The kebabs are cooked when the scallops are opaque and firm and the bacon is crisp. Serve with lemon wedges.

ZURICH KEBABS WITH GARLIC AND SAGE BUTTER

Serves 4

1½ lbs.	calves' liver, cut in 12 pieces
2 tbsp.	finely chopped fresh sage leaves
	Salt
	Freshly ground pepper
12	bacon slices
12	baby onions, peeled
4	skewers

GARLIC AND SAGE BUTTER

½ cup	butter, melted
3	cloves garlic, crushed
1 tbsp.	finely chopped fresh sage leaves

Season liver pieces with sage, salt and pepper. Wrap each piece of liver in a slice of bacon. Thread 3 pieces of meat on each skewer. After each piece of meat, place one onion.

To prepare garlic and sage butter, melt butter. Add garlic and sage. Keep warm.

Cook kebabs over hot coals 8 to 10 minutes, turning frequently and basting with the garlic and sage butter. Just before serving, baste generously.

INDIAN CHICKEN KEBABS

Serves 4

1 lb.	boneless, skinless chicken breasts, cut in cubes
8	bamboo sticks, soaked in cold water for 1 hour

MARINADE

1	medium onion, coarsely chopped
2	cloves garlic, coarsely chopped
2 tsp.	chopped fresh ginger root
2 tbsp.	lemon juice
1/4 cup	plain yogurt
1 tsp.	ground coriander
1 tsp.	garam masala
1 tsp.	salt
1/2 tsp.	ground cumin
1/2 tsp.	cayenne pepper

The day before the barbecue, place onion, garlic and ginger in a blender or food processor. Add lemon juice and blend until smooth. Stir in yogurt. Add coriander, garam masala, salt, cumin and cayenne pepper. Stir well.

Place chicken pieces in a glass or ceramic bowl. Pour marinade over chicken and cover with plastic wrap. Marinate overnight in the refrigerator.

Remove chicken and reserve marinade. Thread chicken on bamboo sticks. Barbecue over glowing coals for 3 to 4 minutes, turning often and basting with marinade.

CLASSIC JAPANESE CHICKEN ON BAMBOO SKEWERS

Serves 4

1 lb.	boneless, skinless chicken breasts, cut in cubes
8	bamboo sticks, soaked in water for 1 hour

SAUCE

¼ cup	molasses
1¼ cups	shoyu (Japanese soy sauce)
½ cup	granulated sugar
1 tbsp.	sake (Japanese wine)

Place molasses, shoyu and sugar in a large heavy saucepan. Stir over medium heat until sugar has dissolved. Bring sauce to the boil, then turn heat to very low. Simmer, uncovered, for 1 hour. Remove from heat. When cool, add sake.

Thread chicken pieces on bamboo sticks. Brush well with sauce. Place on grill over medium-hot coals. Cook about 5 to 8 minutes, basting frequently with sauce and turning often.

Burgers

Burgers are a traditional favorite. You can barbecue them directly on the grill or in a frying pan.

Burgers should be juicy and tender, not dry and rock-hard as they so often are. To make sure your burgers stay moist, choose a ground meat that contains some fat.

Shape your burger patties before your guests arrive. Cover them and place them in the refrigerator until you are ready to barbecue.

If you have unexpected guests, remember you can always extend your meat by adding egg, breadcrumbs, rolled oats or cooked rice.

Remember that burgers shrink on the barbecue. If they are too small, they will dry out quickly.

You can also shape the meat around a skewer like a sausage.

Burgers should always be basted on the barbecue. A light vegetable oil is ideal, or use leftover marinade.

All sorts of mustards, pickles, relishes, sauces and ingredients are good with hamburgers. Don't be afraid to experiment.

SMOKED FISH PATTIES WITH TARTARE SAUCE

Makes 6 burgers

1 lb.	smoked salmon, trout or mackerel
2 cups	milk
1 cup	cooked rice
1/4 lb.	Cheddar cheese, grated
	Freshly ground black pepper
1	egg, lightly beaten
1/2 stalk	celery, finely chopped
2 tbsp.	chopped sweet red pepper
2 tbsp.	finely chopped fresh parsley
1/2 tsp.	chopped fresh dill
1 cup	fresh white breadcrumbs
	Salt
	Grated Parmesan cheese (optional)

TARTARE SAUCE

2 tbsp.	finely chopped capers
2 tbsp.	finely chopped sour gherkins
3/4 cup	Basic Mayonnaise (page 9)
1 cup	very finely chopped mixed fresh herbs (e.g., parsley, dill, sorrel, lemon thyme, tarragon)

Poach fish gently in milk for 10 to 12 minutes. Drain fish and remove skin and bones. Flake fish into small pieces. Cool.

Combine fish, rice, Cheddar cheese, pepper, egg, celery, red pepper, parsley, dill, breadcrumbs and salt. Mix well.

Divide fish mixture into 6 portions and flatten into burgers. Sprinkle with Parmesan cheese. Refrigerate for at least 1 hour.

To make tartare sauce, combine all sauce ingredients. Store in screw-top jar in the refrigerator until ready to serve.

Place burgers on well-oiled barbecue grill over hot coals. Cook for 5 to 6 minutes each side, turning only once. Serve with tartare sauce.

CHICKEN AND ALMOND BURGERS

Makes 6 burgers

1½ lbs.	cooked chicken, finely chopped
1	red pepper, diced
½	onion, finely diced
¼ cup	salted almonds, finely chopped
1 tsp.	ground ginger
	Freshly ground black pepper
	Salt
2	eggs, lightly beaten
1 cup	breadcrumbs
¼ cup	grated Parmesan cheese

Place cooked chicken in a blender or a food processor. Add red pepper, onion, almonds, ginger, pepper and salt. Add beaten eggs and half the breadcrumbs to the chicken mixture. Blend.

Shape the mixture into 6 patties. Combine remaining breadcrumbs with Parmesan cheese. Roll patties in breadcrumb and cheese mixture.

Place patties on a double thickness of oiled foil or in an oiled frying pan. Place foil or pan on barbecue grill above a solid bed of glowing coals. Cook about 6 minutes each side, turning patties once with a metal spatula.

IDAHO BURGERS

Makes 6 to 8 burgers

2	large onions, chopped
2 tbsp.	butter
2 cups	mashed potato, cooled
2	slices bacon, cooked until crisp then finely chopped
	Salt and pepper
1 lb.	lean minced beef
1	clove garlic, crushed

Sauté onions in half the butter until golden. Put onions in a large bowl. Add remaining butter, potato, bacon, salt and pepper.

In a separate bowl, combine beef and garlic. Add to potato mixture and mix thoroughly. Shape into 6 or 8 burgers.

Place burgers in a hinged wire grill. Set on barbecue grill above medium-hot coals. Cook for 6 to 8 minutes each side, or until cooked through. Be careful. These burgers are very fragile.

SPICY LAMB AND APRICOT BURGERS

Makes 6 burgers

¾ cup	dried apricots
2 tbsp.	orange juice
½ cup	catsup
1 tsp.	curry powder
½ tsp.	garam masala
1 tsp.	chili powder
1½ lbs.	ground lamb
½ cup	dry breadcrumbs
¼ cup	finely chopped fresh parsley
½	onion, finely chopped
	Salt

Soak apricots in water for 12 hours. Drain and place in a blender or food processor. Add orange juice and purée.

In a bowl, place apricot purée, catsup, curry powder, garam masala and chili powder. Mix well. Add lamb and mix again. Add breadcrumbs, parsley, onion and salt. Mix, then shape into 6 patties.

Place patties in a hinged wire grill on barbecue over medium-hot coals. Cook for about 6 minutes on each side, turning once.

HONG KONG BURGERS

Makes 8 to 10 burgers

¹/₂	red sweet pepper, finely chopped
¹/₄ cup	black bean sauce (available in Oriental grocery stores)
3	shallots, finely chopped
2	cloves garlic, crushed
2 tbsp.	soy sauce
1 tbsp.	brown sugar
2 tsp.	Worcestershire sauce
1 tsp.	grated fresh ginger root
¹/₂ tsp.	wasabi (Oriental green horseradish sauce)
	Freshly ground black pepper
1¹/₂ lbs.	lean ground beef

In a large bowl, blend sweet pepper, black bean sauce, shallots, garlic, soy sauce, brown sugar, Worcestershire sauce, ginger, wasabi and pepper. Add beef and knead with your fingers or mix with a wooden spoon until sauce has been absorbed.

Shape into 8 to 10 patties. Put patties in a hinged wire grill and place on barbecue over medium-hot coals. Cook 20 minutes in all, turning occasionally.

MEDITERRANEAN BURGERS

Makes 4 burgers

These are delicious served on pita bread.

1 lb.	lean ground beef
12	pimento stuffed olives, finely chopped
1	clove garlic, crushed
2 tbsp.	grated Gruyère cheese
2 tbsp.	lemon juice
1 tbsp.	finely chopped fresh parsley
½ tsp	grated lemon zest
½ tsp.	salt
	Freshly ground black pepper

Place ground beef in a large bowl. Add remaining ingredients and mix well. Shape into 4 patties.

Put burgers in a hinged wire grill and place on barbecue over medium-hot coals. Cook 6 to 8 minutes on each side, turning burgers only once with flat metal spatula.

STARS AND STRIPES BURGERS

Makes 6 burgers

1½ lbs.	lean ground beef
1	onion, finely chopped
1½	cloves garlic, finely chopped
2 tbsp.	catsup
1 tsp.	Worcestershire sauce
	Salt
	Freshly ground pepper
6	hamburger rolls

Put beef in a large bowl. Add onion, garlic, catsup, Worcestershire sauce, salt and pepper. Knead until well blended. Shape meat into 6 patties.

Put patties in a hinged wire grill and place on barbecue over a solid bed of glowing coals. Cook for about 6 minutes on each side, turning only once. When you turn the patty, place the rolls cut-side down on the grill to toast.

Serve with mustard, mayonnaise, catsup or relish. Garnish with sliced onion, tomato, avocado, dill pickles or shredded lettuce.

LAMBURGERS

Makes 4 to 6 burgers

These can be served on a toasted hamburger roll with a tossed salad or on pita bread with tahini.

1½ lbs.	ground lamb
	Juice of ½ lemon
20	stuffed green olives, finely chopped
1	clove garlic, crushed
2 tbsp.	grated onion
2 tbsp.	chopped fresh parsley
1 tsp.	chopped fresh rosemary
1	egg, lightly beaten
	Salt
	Freshly ground pepper
½ tsp.	cayenne pepper

Place minced lamb in a large bowl. Add remaining ingredients and knead mixture until it is no longer wet. Shape into 4 to 6 patties.

Put patties in hinged wire grill and place on barbecue over solid bed of glowing coals. Cook about 10 minutes on each side, turning burgers only once.

HIDDEN TREASURE BURGERS

Makes 4 large burgers

2 lbs.	lean ground beef
1 cup	soft breadcrumbs
1	egg
1 tbsp.	finely chopped fresh parsley
	Salt
	Freshly ground black pepper
	Filling (see suggestions below)

Place beef in a large bowl. Add breadcrumbs, egg, parsley, salt and pepper. Knead well with your fingers.

Divide meat into 8 portions. Shape each portion into a patty and flatten evenly.

Place surprise filling on 4 of the patties. Set 4 remaining patties on top of filling and pinch edges of patties together until completely sealed.

Place patties on an oiled grill over an even bed of hot coals. Cook 10 to 12 minutes on each side, turning once only with a spatula.

FILLING SUGGESTIONS:

Chopped mushrooms sautéed briefly in olive oil and sherry. Drain mushrooms and sprinkle a little chopped parsley over them.

Slice of cheese with cooked bacon.

Chopped onion and finely sliced zucchini sautéed with garlic.

Sliced avocado and cooked bacon.

Sliced hard-boiled egg sprinkled with chopped chives.

Fresh oysters sprinkled with lemon and hot pepper sauce.

GOURMET GRUYÈRE BURGERS

Makes 6 burgers

1	medium onion, finely chopped
1 tbsp.	vegetable oil
1½ lbs.	lean ground beef
1	clove garlic, crushed
	Salt
	Freshly ground black pepper
6	hamburger rolls
⅓ cup	grated Gruyère cheese
	Dijon mustard
	Bacon, fried until crisp and crumbled, for garnish
	Avocado slices for garnish
	Tomato slices for garnish

Sauté onion in oil until it is just browned. Place onion in a bowl, then add ground beef, garlic, salt and pepper.

Shape into 6 patties. Put patties in hinged wire grill and place over a solid bed of glowing coals. Cook about 6 minutes. Turn burgers and cook second side for 4 minutes. Place hamburger rolls cut-side down on the barbecue grill to toast. Top each patty with grated Gruyère cheese and cook for an additional 2 minutes.

Serve burgers on rolls with Dijon mustard, crisp bacon, avocado or sliced tomato.

Spareribs

When we refer to pork side spareribs, we mean the ribs that come from the side of pork. In our opinion, they are more flavorsome than the pork back ribs, which are meatier. However, the choice is yours.

Pork side spareribs have a lot of bones and very little meat. They are also extremely inexpensive per portion.

Since lamb and beef ribs are bigger and meatier than pork ribs, you will not need as many.

Spareribs should be basted and turned frequently so they don't burn.

Provide a big bowl for your guests to put the chewed bones into.

PIQUANT PLUM PORK SPARERIBS

Serves 6

4 lbs.	pork side spareribs

PLUM SAUCE

14 oz. can	purple plums
½ cup	frozen orange juice concentrate
1 tbsp.	bottled Chinese plum sauce
½ tsp.	Worcestershire sauce
2	cloves garlic, crushed

Place ribs in a shallow ceramic or glass dish so they lie flat.

Drain the plums and reserve the syrup. Force plums through a sieve or purée them in a blender. Add the reserved syrup, orange juice concentrate, plum sauce, Worcestershire sauce and garlic. Mix well, then pour over ribs. Marinate ribs for at least 1 hour.

Drain ribs and reserve marinade. Place ribs on a well-oiled grill over medium-hot coals. Brush them with half the plum sauce and cook for 10 minutes. Turn ribs carefully, then brush with the remaining sauce. Cook for a further 20 minutes, or until tender.

VINDALOO LAMB RIBS

Serves 8

| 4 lbs. | breast of lamb ribs, divided in individual ribs (28 to 30 ribs) |
| | Fresh coriander sprigs for garnish |

PASTE

2 tsp.	whole cardamon pods
1 tbsp.	whole cumin seeds
4 to 6	hot dried chilies
¾ cup	white wine vinegar
1 tbsp.	curry powder
2 tsp.	brown sugar
1 tsp.	ground cinnamon
1 tsp.	salt
2	medium onions, peeled and sliced into rings
¼ cup	vegetable oil
2 to 3 tbsp.	water

The day before the barbecue, place lamb ribs in a shallow ceramic or glass dish.

Put the cardamon pods, cumin seeds and chilies in a coffee or spice grinder and grind until you have a fine powder. Put the ground spices in a bowl. Add vinegar, curry powder, brown sugar, cinnamon and salt. Mix well and set aside.

Fry onion rings in oil until they are brown and crisp. Remove with slotted spoon. Put the fried onions in a blender or food processor. Add water and purée the onions. Add onion purée to ground spices in bowl and mix well.

Coat the lamb ribs well with half the curry paste. Reserve other half of paste. Cover lamb ribs with plastic wrap and refrigerate overnight.

Let lamb ribs come back to room temperature. Thin the reserved curry paste with a little oil so you can brush it on the ribs easily.

Place ribs on a well-oiled grill above medium-hot coals. Cook 20 to 30 minutes, brushing frequently with thinned curry paste and turning every 10 minutes. Garnish with coriander and serve.

APRICOT PORK SPARERIBS

Serves 4

4 lbs.   pork side spareribs

MARINADE

19 oz. can	apricot halves, drained
1 cup	crushed pineapple
¼ cup	apricot brandy
¼ cup	brown sugar
3 tbsp.	white vinegar
1 tbsp.	soy sauce
2 tsp.	ground cinnamon
½ tsp.	ground ginger

The day before the barbecue, place apricots in a blender. Process until smooth. Place apricot purée in a saucepan and add remaining marinade ingredients. Bring to a boil. Reduce heat and simmer for 5 minutes, stirring occasionally. Let cool.

Place pork ribs in a glass or ceramic dish large enough for the sheets of ribs to lie flat. Pour marinade over ribs. Cover with plastic wrap and refrigerate overnight. Turn a few times.

Remove ribs. Reserve marinade for basting.

Grill ribs over medium-hot coals for 15 to 20 minutes, basting and turning frequently. Cut ribs into serving pieces.

ORIENTAL GARLIC PORK SPARERIBS

Serves 4

| 2 lbs. | pork side spareribs |

MARINADE

⅓ cup	dry sherry
⅓ cup	sesame oil
1 tbsp.	brown sugar
2 tsp.	grated fresh ginger root
1 tsp.	Chinese five-spice powder
¼ tsp.	freshly ground black pepper
6	cloves garlic, crushed
	Salt

The day before the barbecue, place spareribs in a glass or ceramic dish. Combine marinade ingredients and pour over the ribs. Cover with plastic wrap. Marinate in the refrigerator overnight, turning meat occasionally.

The next day, remove ribs and reserve marinade. Place ribs on a grill over medium-hot coals. Baste frequently with marinade and turn ribs often. Barbecue for 15 to 20 minutes, or until cooked. Divide meat into individual servings.

CHILI PORK SPARERIBS

Serves 6

4 lbs.	pork side spareribs

MARINADE

½ cup	soy sauce
¼ cup	hot water
¼ cup	brown sugar
2 tbsp.	dry sherry
2	cloves garlic, crushed
1 tbsp.	catsup
1 tsp.	grated fresh ginger root
1 tsp.	chili sauce

The day before the barbecue, place ribs in a glass or ceramic dish large enough to hold them flat. Mix marinade ingredients together and pour over ribs. Cover with plastic wrap and refrigerate overnight, basting ribs occasionally.

Remove ribs from dish. Reserve marinade.

Place ribs on a well-oiled grill over medium-hot coals. Brush with marinade. Cook for 15 to 20 minutes, turning and basting often.

SWEET AND SOUR PORK SPARERIBS

Serves 4

4 lbs.	pork side spareribs

MARINADE

2 tbsp.	brown sugar
1/4 cup	frozen orange juice concentrate
2 tbsp.	honey
2 tbsp.	bottled barbecue sauce
1 tbsp.	white vinegar
	Juice of 1/2 lemon
1/2 cup	pineapple juice
2	cloves garlic, crushed
1 tbsp.	grated fresh ginger root

To prepare the marinade, place the brown sugar in a large bowl. Blend in orange juice, honey, barbecue sauce, vinegar and lemon juice. Mix in pineapple juice, garlic and ginger.

Place the ribs in a shallow glass or ceramic dish. Pour marinade over ribs and marinate for 1 to 2 hours, turning ribs occasionally.

Remove ribs. Set aside marinade.

Place ribs on a well-oiled grill over medium-hot coals. Cook for 15 to 20 minutes, brushing often with the marinade and turning every 5 minutes.

HOT CHILI BEEF RIBS

Serves 6

4 lbs.	beef spareribs
3 or 4	cloves garlic, crushed
1/3 cup	Dijon mustard
2 tsp.	chili powder
1 tsp.	sugar
	Hot pepper sauce
	Pinch salt

Place beef ribs on a large flat platter. Combine the rest of the ingredients and spread evenly over the beef ribs.

Place ribs on an oiled grill over fairly hot coals. Cook 30 to 45 minutes, turning often. Divide the ribs into serving portions.

LAMB RIBS IN CITRUS-DILL MARINADE

Serves 4

2^1/$_2$ lbs.	breast of lamb ribs

MARINADE

^{1}/$_2$ cup	lemon juice
^{1}/$_2$ cup	olive oil
^{1}/$_2$ cup	chopped fresh dill
^{1}/$_4$ cup	orange juice
2 tbsp.	Dijon mustard
	Salt
	Freshly ground black pepper

Trim excess fat from lamb. Place ribs in a shallow glass or ceramic dish in a single layer. Combine marinade ingredients. Pour marinade over the lamb, making sure meat is well coated. Cover the dish and refrigerate overnight, basting ribs occasionally.

Drain lamb and reserve marinade. Barbecue lamb over hot coals, basting frequently, for about 16 to 18 minutes, turning every 2 minutes. Cut ribs into serving portions.

Vegetables

Hot barbecued vegetables make perfect accompaniments to fish, meat and poultry.

Always buy fresh vegetables.

When you wrap vegetables in foil, remember to leave room for steam to expand. Always place the vegetables on the shiny side of the foil.

If you are cooking vegetables on the grill without foil, baste them frequently.

Many vegetables already have their own protective skins and are therefore most suitable for barbecuing. For example, pumpkins, potatoes, sweet potatoes, onions and eggplant can be cooked in their skins.

If you are threading vegetables onto skewers, cut the ones that require a long cooking time into small pieces and the ones that cook quickly into larger pieces.

Don't overcook vegetables. They should not be mushy; they should be firm to the touch.

Tahitian Prawns (p. 91)

ITALIAN EGGPLANT WITH PESTO

Serves 8

3	large eggplants
	Salt
	Olive oil
	Freshly ground pepper

PESTO

3	cloves garlic
1 cup	fresh basil leaves
2 tbsp.	pine nuts
1/4 cup	olive oil

Remove stalks and cut eggplants into thick diagonal slices. Place slices in a colander and sprinkle with salt. Leave for 30 minutes.

To make the pesto, place garlic, basil and pine nuts in a blender or food processor. Blend to a fine paste. With the motor running, gradually add olive oil. Set aside.

When barbecue coals are ready, brush the grill with oil. Place eggplant on grill, then brush with olive oil and season with salt and pepper. Barbecue for 2 to 3 minutes on each side, brushing occasionally with oil. Serve with pesto.

Italian Eggplant with Pesto

POMMES DE TERRE ROQUEFORTS

Serves 6

These potatoes are cooked in the oven.

6	large potatoes
	Vegetable oil
⅓ cup	sour cream
¼ cup	milk
5 oz.	Roquefort cheese, crumbled
2 tbsp.	chopped parsley
1 tsp.	salt
	Freshly ground black pepper
¼ cup	butter
1 tbsp.	chopped chives

Preheat oven to 450°F. (225°C). Wash potatoes and pat dry. Rub potato skins with oil and prick several times. Place in hot oven for 45 to 60 minutes or until tender.

Cut potatoes in half and scoop out pulp. Do not break the skins.

Mash pulp well. Add sour cream and milk. Beat until smooth. Stir in cheese, setting aside enough for the garnish. Add parsley, salt and pepper.

Place mashed potato mixture back in potato shells, mounding slightly. Dot each potato with butter. Return to oven for 10 minutes.

Garnish with chopped chives and reserved Roquefort cheese. Serve hot.

ROASTED CORN ON THE COB IN HERB AND MUSTARD BUTTER

Serves 8

8 ears	corn

HERB AND MUSTARD BUTTER

1 cup	unsalted butter, softened
2 tbsp.	finely chopped parsley
2 tbsp.	finely chopped chives
2 tbsp.	finely chopped shallots
2 tsp.	fresh lemon juice
1 tsp.	Dijon mustard
½ tsp.	salt
	Freshly ground black pepper

Peel back corn husks but do not remove them. Remove silk. Soak the ears of corn in water.

Combine all herb and mustard butter ingredients. Beat until fluffy and soft. Spread each ear of corn with a little herb and mustard butter. Replace husks and wrap ears of corn in foil.

Roast corn on a grill over hot glowing coals for 10 to 15 minutes, turning often. Unwrap foil. Remove husks and serve with reserved herb and mustard butter.

VEGETABLE BROCHETTES WITH GARLIC BUTTER

Serves 4

Use any of the vegetables listed. You will need enough for eight bamboo skewers.

	Mushroom caps
	Baby onions
	Cherry tomatoes
	Zucchini, cut in thick slices
	Eggplant, cut in cubes
	Red or green pepper, cut in squares
	Radishes
8	strips bacon
8	bamboo skewers, soaked in water for 1 hour

BASTE

½ cup	unsalted butter, melted
1 or 2	cloves garlic, crushed
	Finely chopped fresh parsley
	Freshly ground black pepper
	Salt

Thread vegetables and bacon strips on skewers. Weave bacon under and over vegetables.

Combine baste ingredients and brush over vegetables.

Place skewers on an oiled grill over hot coals. Barbecue until vegetables are cooked to your liking and bacon is crisp. Turn and baste frequently.

NOTE: You can marinate any of the vegetables in a vinaigrette for 2 or 3 hours before cooking. Baste with melted butter while cooking.

ZUCCHINI SOUFFLÉS

Serves 4

8	large zucchini
⅓ cup	butter
¼ tsp.	salt
	Freshly ground pepper
¼ cup	all-purpose flour
¾ cup	milk
3	eggs, separated
	Pinch cayenne pepper
	Pinch dry mustard
	Pinch nutmeg
½ cup	freshly grated Parmesan cheese
8½ × 12½ inch	glass baking dish

Wash zucchini, cut lengthwise into halves. Scoop out flesh of each zucchini half, leaving a shell. Chop flesh and set aside. Arrange zucchini shells in greased baking dish.

In a large saucepan, heat a little of the butter. Add chopped zucchini; sauté about 10 minutes, stirring constantly, until liquid is reduced and mixture resembles a thick purée. Season with salt and pepper to taste.

In a heavy saucepan, heat remaining butter; add flour, stirring constantly about 1 minute until mixture is well blended and a smooth paste forms. Remove saucepan from heat, add milk a little at a time, whisking constantly until mixture is well blended. Place sauce back on low heat, stirring constantly about 2 minutes until a thick sauce forms. Stir in egg yolks, one at a time, beating until each yolk is well blended. Add zucchini pulp, cayenne, mustard, nutmeg and grated Parmesan cheese; stir well, remove from heat. In a mixer bowl, beat egg whites about 3 minutes until stiff peaks form. Fold whites into warm zucchini mixture. Spoon this mixture into zucchini shells. Bake in a 350°F. (180°C) oven for 25 minutes or until puffed and golden. Serve immediately.

SWEET POTATO CHIPS

These should be cooked in advance in your kitchen.

1 lb.   medium sweet potatoes
               Vegetable oil for deep-frying
               Salt

Peel sweet potatoes and rinse them well. Cut potatoes into paper-thin slices. Wash slices; dry each slice well.

In a deep saucepan or frying pan, heat oil until a potato slice sizzles when dropped in.

Place sliced potatoes in the pan in batches, being careful not to splash the hot oil. Deep-fry for 20 minutes or until chips are crisp and deep orange in color. They will curl up a little.

Remove chips from oil and place on paper towels to drain thoroughly. If necessary, pat with another paper towel to make sure all oil is removed. Sprinkle with salt.

BAKED POTATOES WITH CAVIAR

Serves 6

6	potatoes
2 tbsp.	vegetable oil
	Salt
¼ cup	butter
¼ cup	sour cream
1 tbsp.	black caviar
1 tbsp.	red caviar
	Freshly ground black pepper

Scrub potatoes and prick skins all over with a fork. Brush each potato with oil and sprinkle salt over the skins.

Wrap each potato in a double thickness of aluminum foil and place directly into hot coals. Cook 50 minutes to 1 hour. Test by inserting a metal skewer through foil into potato: potato is done when it is tender.

Unwrap potatoes. Cut a deep cross in the top of each potato. Put a pat of butter on each potato. Add a dollop of sour cream and top with black and red caviar. Grind a little black pepper over each potato and serve.

NOTE: You can use finely chopped chives, dill or cooked bacon bits instead of caviar.

RATATOUILLE PROVENÇALE

Serves 8

This dish is cooked in the kitchen and served cold at the barbecue.

⅓ cup	olive oil
2	large onions, sliced
2	large eggplants, unpeeled, cubed
2	green peppers, trimmed and sliced
6	medium zucchini, unpeeled, sliced
2	cloves garlic, crushed
1 lb.	tomatoes, blanched, peeled and chopped
	Freshly ground black pepper
	Salt
2 tbsp.	finely chopped fresh parsley
1 tbsp.	finely chopped fresh oregano
2 tsp.	finely chopped fresh marjoram
2 tsp.	finely chopped fresh basil

Heat olive oil in the bottom of a heavy casserole. Add onions and sauté until transparent.

Add eggplant cubes, green pepper and zucchini. Stir well. Cover and simmer for 10 minutes. Stir in garlic and tomatoes.

Season to taste with pepper and salt. Continue cooking until tomatoes are soft. Cover and simmer for another 10 to 15 minutes.

Add parsley, oregano, marjoram and basil. Cover and simmer over low heat for 8 to 10 minutes. Chill. Serve cold.

ASPARAGI ROMANO

Serves 4

1 lb.	tender fresh asparagus
2 tbsp.	grated Romano cheese
¼ cup	butter, melted
	Salt
	Freshly ground black pepper

Wash asparagus. Cut off rough ends and remove any scaly parts. Place in rapidly boiling salted water for about 1 minute and 30 seconds.

Divide asparagus into 4 portions. Place each portion on a layer of aluminum foil. Combine Romano cheese and melted butter. Pour over asparagus and season to taste with salt and pepper.

Seal foil loosely. Place on barbecue grill over medium-hot coals for 8 to 10 minutes. Do not turn over. Cut open foil with scissors and serve immediately.

Salads

On a hot day there is nothing better than a big fresh tossed salad.

Plan on serving two or three to provide color and texture.

Choose the salads to fit the style of barbecue you are having. Try to plan it so that the nationalities blend. For example, serve the Light Japanese Salad (page 140) with Classic Japanese Chicken on Bamboo Skewers (page 101).

Always use fresh fruits and vegetables and refrigerate your salads until serving time. They can be ruined if they are unintentionally left in the sun.

Remember to wash and dry your ingredients (where necessary), then refrigerate in a freezer bag to make sure they are crisp.

Unless the salad is marinated, add the dressing and toss the salad just before serving.

Remember that fresh raw vegetables and fruits contain much more nutrition than cooked ones.

SCALLOPS AND SNOW PEA SALAD WITH BASIL MAYONNAISE

Serves 6

1 lb.	fresh scallops
½ cup	dry white wine
½ lb.	snow peas
1	avocado, halved, peeled and sliced
1	romaine lettuce
¼	English cucumber, sliced
2	shallots, chopped, for garnish
3	hard-boiled eggs, sliced, for garnish
1 tbsp.	chopped fresh basil for garnish

BASIL MAYONNAISE

1 cup	finely chopped fresh basil
3	cloves garlic, crushed
3/4 cup	Basic Mayonnaise (page 9)
	Salt
	Freshly ground black pepper

Poach the scallops in wine for 30 seconds. Set aside to cool.

Cut ends off the snow peas. Blanch whole in salted boiling water for 10 seconds. Place quickly under cold running water, then set aside to cool.

To prepare basil mayonnaise: combine all mayonnaise ingredients. Refrigerate.

Mix scallops and snow peas with avocado slices. Fold in the basil mayonnaise. Chill.

At serving time, line a salad bowl with romaine leaves. Place the scallop and mayonnaise mixture in the center of the leaves. Add cucumber, then garnish with shallots, eggs and basil.

HUNGARIAN GOURMET POTATO SALAD

Serves 6

2 lbs.	new potatoes
6	green onions, finely chopped
4	stalks celery, finely chopped
2	medium-sized dill pickles, thinly sliced
1	large sour green apple, peeled, cored and finely chopped
½ cup	sour cream
¼ cup	white vinegar
1 tsp.	salt
	Freshly ground black pepper
½ tsp.	paprika
2 tbsp.	finely chopped fresh parsley

Boil unpeeled potatoes in lightly salted water for 10 to 15 minutes. Drain and cool. When cool enough to handle but still warm, peel and cut into halves.

Put warm potatoes in a large salad bowl. Add green onions, celery, dill pickles and apple.

Mix the sour cream with the vinegar. Pour over the warm potatoes and vegetables. Season to taste. Sprinkle paprika over salad. Toss well. Garnish with parsley.

ITALIAN FLORET SALAD

Serves 6

1	large red sweet pepper
1 tbsp.	olive oil
½ lb.	broccoli
½ lb.	cauliflower
5	anchovy fillets, chopped
12	Italian black olives

DRESSING

6 tbsp.	olive oil
3 tbsp.	lemon juice
	Salt
	Freshly ground black pepper

GARNISH

1 tbsp.	capers, drained
2 tbsp.	finely chopped fresh parsley

Cut red pepper in half lengthwise. Remove seeds and ribs. Rub olive oil on skin and grill for a few minutes. Set aside to cool. Peel off skin and slice thinly.

Cut broccoli and cauliflower into separate florets. Place florets in a saucepan of rapidly boiling salted water for about 3 minutes. Drain and rinse quickly under cold running water.

Put red pepper, broccoli and cauliflower into a glass salad bowl. Add anchovy fillets and olives.

Mix the dressing ingredients together. Pour over vegetables. Cover and refrigerate for about 4 hours.

Before serving, garnish with capers and parsley.

SRI LANKAN SALAD

Serves 4

6	large firm tomatoes
2 tbsp.	lime juice
	Salt
3	shallots, finely chopped
1/2	green pepper, finely chopped
1	hot chili pepper, seeded and finely chopped
1/4 cup	coconut cream
2 tbsp.	crumbled Bombay duck (available at Oriental grocery stores)

Immerse tomatoes for a few seconds in boiling water. Place under cold running water, then remove skins. (They should slip off easily.) Cut tomatoes in half. Remove and discard seeds. Chop tomatoes into small pieces and place in a salad bowl.

Add lime juice, salt, shallots, green pepper and chili. Pour coconut cream over vegetables. Toss well. Just before serving, sprinkle with Bombay duck.

SOUTH PACIFIC SALAD

Serves 6

2	mangoes, peeled and sliced
½	small ripe pineapple, peeled, cored and cubed
1	cucumber, peeled and sliced thinly
½ lb.	green beans, blanched and halved
¼ lb.	cooked prawns, shelled and deveined
1	pear, cored and chopped
¼ lb.	roasted peanuts for garnish

LEMON AND LIME DRESSING

⅔ cup	peanut oil
⅓ cup	lemon and lime juice, mixed
1 tsp.	granulated sugar
2	cloves garlic, crushed
½ tsp.	dry English mustard
	Zest of ½ lime
	Zest of ½ lemon
	Salt
	Freshly ground black pepper

Make dressing by combining all dressing ingredients in a jar. Let stand at room temperature for 2 hours.

In a large bowl, combine mangoes, pineapple, cucumber, beans, prawns and pear. Pour half the dressing over salad and toss well. Place in the refrigerator for 1 hour.

Drain salad and transfer to a serving platter. Pour on the rest of the dressing and garnish with roasted peanuts.

LIGHT JAPANESE SALAD

Serves 4

2	cucumbers, peeled and thinly sliced
6	shallots, finely chopped
½ lb.	bean sprouts
2 tbsp.	sesame seeds for garnish

JAPANESE DRESSING

2 tbsp.	rice wine vinegar (available at Oriental grocery stores)
2 tbsp.	vegetable oil
1 tbsp.	brown sugar
1 tbsp.	shoyu (Japanese soy sauce)
1 tsp.	sesame oil
1 tsp.	wasabi (Japanese horseradish paste)
1	clove garlic, crushed

Put the cucumbers, shallots and bean sprouts in a glass or ceramic bowl.

Combine dressing ingredients. Pour over salad and toss well. Cover with plastic wrap and refrigerate for at least 2 hours.

Garnish with sesame seeds before serving.

Light Japanese Salad

SALADE VERTE

Serves 6

12	young Belgian endive leaves
1 head	romaine lettuce
½ head	curly endive or chicory
2	firm pears
1	large avocado
12	green pitted olives
1 cup	alfalfa sprouts
2 tbsp.	finely chopped fresh parsley

DRESSING

1/3 cup	olive oil
2 tbsp.	white wine vinegar
1 tsp.	granulated sugar
1/2 tsp.	dry mustard
	Salt
	Freshly ground black pepper
1 tbsp.	finely chopped shallots

Wash the Belgian endive, lettuce and curly endive well. Dry thoroughly. Tear into bite-sized pieces and place in a large salad bowl.

Peel, core and slice the pears. Add to salad bowl. Peel avocado. Cut in half and remove the pit. Slice and add to salad bowl. Add olives, alfalfa sprouts and parsley.

Mix together all dressing ingredients. Pour over salad and toss gently, making sure all ingredients are coated. Serve immediately.

French Apple Crumble (p. 155)

SALADE NIÇOISE

Serves 6

½ lb.	green beans
½ lb.	cooked artichoke hearts, cut in halves
½	medium onion, thinly sliced
6½ oz. can	solid tuna, drained and broken in chunks
2 tbsp.	chopped basil
12	cherry tomatoes
12	pitted black olives
½	green pepper, sliced
½	sweet red pepper, sliced
½	romaine lettuce, washed and well dried
3	hard-boiled eggs, shelled and quartered, for garnish
1 tin	anchovies, drained, for garnish
½ cup	finely chopped fresh parsley, for garnish

DRESSING

¾ cup	olive oil
⅓ cup	white vinegar
1 tsp.	dry mustard
3	cloves garlic, sliced
	Salt
	Freshly ground black pepper

The night before, combine dressing ingredients in a glass jar. Shake well and leave for 12 hours at room temperature. Before serving, remove garlic slices.

The next day, immerse beans in boiling water for 2 or 3 minutes. Place under cold running water, then drain and cool. Combine cooled beans, artichoke hearts and onion with one-third of the salad dressing. Marinate in the refrigerator for 1 or 2 hours. Toss 2 or 3 times while marinating.

In another bowl, mix tuna, basil, tomatoes, olives and peppers. Marinate in one-third of the dressing for 1 or 2 hours.

Drain both bowls of marinated vegetables. Line a salad bowl with lettuce leaves. Spoon the bean, artichoke and onion mixture in the center of the salad bowl. Top with the tuna and tomato mixture. Garnish with eggs, anchovies and parsley. Drizzle the remaining one-third of the dressing over the salad and serve.

SHRIMP AND AVOCADO SALAD

Serves 4

4	lettuce leaves
1 lb.	small cooked shrimp, shelled and deveined
2 tbsp.	finely chopped celery
2	hard-boiled eggs, finely chopped
2 tbsp.	finely chopped red sweet pepper
2	shallots, finely chopped
1/4 cup	Basic Mayonnaise (page 9)
1/4 tsp.	curry powder
2	avocados
	Juice of 1/2 lemon
	Freshly ground black pepper

Wash and dry lettuce leaves and set them on 4 individual plates.

Combine shrimp, celery, eggs, red pepper and shallots. In a separate bowl, combine mayonnaise and curry powder. Pour over shrimp mixture and toss to coat. Spoon mixture on lettuce leaves.

Peel avocados and cut in half. Remove pits. Place avocados cut-side down on a chopping board and slice into thin slices. Allowing half an avocado per salad portion, lay slices beside the shrimp mixture.

Sprinkle avocado with lemon juice and plenty of freshly ground black pepper.

MEXICAN SALAD WITH AVOCADO DRESSING

Serves 6

1	ripe avocado
1	red sweet pepper, chopped
1	green pepper, chopped
1	medium onion, chopped
2	medium tomatoes, chopped
2 stalks	celery, chopped
3	hard-boiled eggs, peeled and sliced
½ tsp.	salt
4	slices bacon, cooked until crisp, then crumbled

AVOCADO DRESSING

3	dried chilies, crumbled, or
2	hot fresh chilies, chopped
¾ cup	olive oil
⅓ cup	white vinegar
2	cloves garlic, crushed
4 drops	hot pepper sauce
	Salt

The night before, combine dressing ingredients in a jar. Leave overnight at room temperature.

The next day, strain the dressing; discard chilies and garlic. Set aside a little of the dressing. Pour the rest of the dressing into the bottom of a salad bowl. Cut avocado in half and remove pit. Mash the pulp of half the avocado into the dressing and beat until smooth.

Put peppers, onion, tomatoes, celery, egg and salt in the salad bowl on top of the dressing. Toss until well coated, then add bacon.

Dice remaining avocado half. Add it to the salad and sprinkle with reserved dressing.

PAPAYA BARBADOS

Serves 6

3 tbsp.	seedless raisins
1 tbsp.	rum
3	small papayas, halved and seeded
	Juice of 2 limes
1 cup	Basic Mayonnaise (page 9)
1 tsp.	curry powder
½ lb.	cooked boneless, skinless chicken breasts, diced
1	mango, peeled and diced
2 tbsp.	shredded fresh coconut
2 tbsp.	unsalted peanuts, toasted

Cover raisins with rum. Let stand for about 1 hour.

In a separate bowl, sprinkle papaya halves with lime juice.

In a third bowl, combine mayonnaise and curry powder. Add raisins, chicken and mango.

Place papaya halves on a platter. Spoon chicken mixture onto papaya and garnish with coconut and toasted peanuts.

FRESH FIG SALAD WITH HONEY AND LIME DRESSING

Serves 8

1 lb.	white cabbage, shredded
1 lb.	raw carrots, grated
¼ lb.	hazelnuts, blanched and peeled
2	large green apples, peeled, cored and diced
½ lb.	fresh figs, trimmed
	Handful watercress
	Toasted almonds to garnish

HONEY AND LIME DRESSING

⅔ cup	olive oil
⅓ cup	lime juice
2 tbsp.	honey
1 tsp.	prepared English mustard
½ tsp.	salt
	Freshly ground black pepper

Toss all salad ingredients together. Cover and refrigerate until ready to use.

Combine all dressing ingredients in a jar. Shake until well mixed. Pour into bottom of salad bowl. Add salad ingredients and toss.

CAESAR SALAD WITH GARLIC CROUTONS

Serves 12

1 cup	olive oil
2	cloves garlic, crushed
½ loaf	stale white bread
3 heads	romaine lettuce
½ lb.	Parmesan cheese, freshly grated
¼ tsp.	salt
¼ tsp.	dry mustard
	Freshly ground black pepper
⅓ cup	lemon juice
2	eggs, boiled for 1 minute then lightly beaten
	Dash Worcestershire sauce
2 oz. can	anchovy fillets, drained

The night before, pour olive oil in a jar. Add garlic. Cover and let stand overnight.

The next day, cut stale bread into cubes. Sauté cubes in one-quarter of the garlic oil until golden brown. Drain on paper towels.

Wash romaine lettuce and dry well. Tear into bite-sized pieces and place in a large salad bowl. Combine cheese, salt, mustard and pepper. Sprinkle cheese mixture over lettuce. Toss well.

Beat the lemon juice into the eggs a little at a time. Add Worcestershire sauce. Mix well. Pour one-third of the egg mixture over the lettuce. Toss gently. Repeat twice, adding anchovies and croutons during the last tossing.

Serve immediately.

GREEK BEAN AND FETA SALAD WITH TAHINI DRESSING

Serves 6

1 lb.	green beans
1	red sweet pepper, sliced
1	small onion, sliced in thin rings
⅓ lb.	cherry tomatoes
2 tbsp.	finely chopped fresh parsley
1 tbsp.	chopped fresh oregano
1 tbsp.	chopped Greek black olives
2 oz.	Feta cheese, crumbled

TAHINI DRESSING

⅓ cup	olive oil
2 tbsp.	lemon juice
2 tsp.	tahini (crushed sesame seed paste)
1	clove garlic, crushed
½ tsp.	granulated sugar

Wash beans and remove ends. Place beans and red pepper in boiling salted water for 1 or 2 minutes. Place under cold water. Drain. Arrange on flat serving dish.

Mix the dressing ingredients together and pour over warm vegetables. Add sliced onion and cherry tomatoes.

Sprinkle with parsley and oregano, then garnish with olives and Feta cheese.

SPINACH SALAD

Serves 6

1 lb.	fresh young spinach leaves
¼ lb.	small mushrooms
6	slices bacon
⅓ cup	olive oil
2 tbsp.	lemon juice
½ tsp.	dry mustard
	Salt
	Freshly ground pepper
6	artichoke hearts, quartered

Wash the spinach thoroughly. Drain and dry well. Tear leaves into bite-sized pieces. Place in a large wooden salad bowl.

Clean mushrooms. Slice and add to salad bowl.

Fry bacon until crisp. Drain on paper towels, then crumble. Place half the bacon in the salad bowl. Reserve the rest.

In a separate small bowl, mix oil, lemon juice, mustard, salt and pepper. Blend and pour over salad. Toss well.

Garnish salad with artichoke hearts and remaining crumbled bacon. Serve immediately.

INDONESIAN GADO GADO WITH PEANUT DRESSING

Serves 6

1	onion, sliced in rings
1 tbsp.	peanut oil
⅔ lb.	green beans, sliced
½ head	lettuce, shredded
½ lb.	bean sprouts
¼ cup	fresh pineapple, chopped
1	cucumber, peeled and sliced
2	potatoes, peeled, boiled and sliced
3	hard-boiled eggs, peeled and sliced
1 tbsp.	dry roasted peanuts
	Fresh coriander
	Shrimp crackers

PEANUT DRESSING

¼ cup	peanut oil
1	onion, very finely chopped
2	red chilies, finely chopped
2	cloves garlic, crushed
	Salt
½ cup	smooth peanut butter
1¼ cups	coconut cream
1 tbsp.	lemon juice
½ tsp.	grated fresh ginger root
1 tsp.	brown sugar

Sauté onion rings in peanut oil until crisp. Drain on paper towels.

Cook green beans in boiling salted water until just tender. Drain.

Cover a large serving platter with shredded lettuce. Arrange cooked beans, bean sprouts, pineapple, cucumber and potatoes on lettuce. Add cooled fried onion rings, eggs and peanuts. Set aside.

To make dressing, heat peanut oil in a frying pan. Sauté onion, chilies and garlic until fragrant. Add salt. Stir in peanut butter and coconut cream. Bring to a boil. Add the lemon juice, ginger and brown sugar. Turn down heat and simmer for 1 or 2 minutes, stirring.

Pour dressing over salad. Garnish with coriander and shrimp crackers.

GINGERED MELON AND SHRIMP SALAD

Serves 4

This makes a delicious and unusual salad or appetizer.

1	musk melon or cantaloupe
1	honeydew melon
1/3 cup	dry white wine
2 tsp.	grated fresh ginger root
1 cup	whipping cream
1 tsp.	ground nutmeg
2 tsp.	cinnamon and granulated sugar, mixed
1 1/2 lbs.	medium-sized cooked shrimp, shelled and deveined
	Handful fresh mint leaves

Cut melons in half and remove seeds. Using a melon baller, scoop out flesh. Reserve melon shells. In a large bowl, combine wine and ginger. Add melon balls and refrigerate for 1 hour.

Beat cream until soft peaks form. Add nutmeg and cinnamon-sugar. Fold in gingered melon balls and shrimp, making sure they are well coated with cream and spice mixture. Spoon into reserved melon shells. Garnish with fresh mint leaves.

Desserts

Desserts are a wonderful way to end a barbecue.

Most of these desserts can be prepared well in advance of the barbecue. Only one of our recipes requires barbecue cooking because we feel desserts are easier if they are prepared ahead of time. However, if you would prefer to use a barbecued dessert, here are a few suggestions:

- Place sliced apples in foil with butter, cinnamon and sugar. Barbecue and serve with whipped cream.
- Wrap peeled bananas in foil with brown sugar, butter and sultanas.
- Put sliced pears in foil with a little water and sugar. Barbecue, then top with toasted almonds and whipped cream.
- Prepare mixed-fruit skewers and baste them with butter and orange juice.

FRENCH APPLE CRUMBLE

Serves 6

¾ cup	water
1	egg, slightly beaten
	Juice of 1 lemon
2 lbs.	peeled, cored and
	sliced green apples
½ cup	sugar
2 tsp.	cinnamon
1½ tsp.	baking powder
½ cup	slivered almonds, toasted
½ cup	combination of sultanas, currants and raisins
	Grand Marnier liqueur

TOPPING

½ cup	self-raising flour
½ cup	firmly packed brown sugar
½ cup	oatmeal
2 tsp.	cinnamon
¼ tsp.	salt
2 tsp.	grated lemon zest
¼ cup	butter
	Whipped cream
9 inch	square baking dish

In a large bowl, combine water, egg and lemon juice. Add apples, and toss gently to coat with lemon juice mixture.

In another bowl, combine sugar, cinnamon, baking powder, almonds and mixed fruit; mix well. Pour over apple mixture, stir well. Transfer to a lightly greased deep square baking dish. Pour Grand Marnier over apple mixture.

To make topping: in a bowl, combine flour, sugar, oatmeal, cinnamon, salt and lemon zest. Add butter, mix well until mixture resembles coarse crumbs. Spoon topping over apple mixture, patting down firmly. Bake in a 350°F. (180°C) oven for 1 hour until bubbly. Serve with dollops of whipped cream. Makes 8 to 10 servings.

STUFFED PEACHES WITH RASPBERRY PURÉE

Serves 4

2 pints	raspberries
¼ lb.	marshmallows, finely chopped
1 cup	sour cream
2 tbsp.	Grand Marnier (optional)
¼ cup	granulated sugar
4	ripe peaches

Mix together half the raspberries, the marshmallows, sour cream, Grand Marnier and one-half of the sugar.

Place remaining raspberries in a blender. Add remaining sugar and process until smooth. Strain to remove seeds.

Place peaches in boiling water for about 30 seconds. Remove and place under cold running water. Peel. Cut peaches in half and remove pits. Place some raspberry cream in the center of each peach.

Pour one-quarter of raspberry purée into the middle of each serving plate. Place 2 peach halves on each plate and serve.

MAPLE PECAN PIE

Makes one pie

PASTRY

1 cup	all-purpose flour
	Pinch salt
6 tbsp.	unsalted butter
¼ cup	iced water

FILLING

¼ cup	soft butter
1 cup	lightly packed brown sugar
	Pinch salt
⅓ cup	corn syrup
⅓ cup	maple syrup
3	eggs, beaten
1 tsp.	vanilla extract
¼ lb.	pecan halves

Preheat oven to 450°F. (230°C).

Sift together flour and salt. Cut butter into flour and salt until the mixture has the texture of fine crumbs. Mix in just enough water to form a stiff dough. Turn onto lightly floured surface and roll out. Place crust in pie plate. Refrigerate for 1 hour.

To make filling, cream butter with sugar and salt. Add corn syrup, maple syrup, eggs and vanilla. Stir.

Arrange pecan halves in a circular pattern on prepared pie crust. Pour syrup mixture over pecans. Bake for 10 minutes. Reduce heat to 350°F.(180°C) and bake for a further 30 to 40 minutes, or until set.

AMBROSIA TREAT

Serves 6

1	pineapple, peeled and cored
2 tbsp.	confectioners sugar
3	ripe bananas, peeled and sliced
¼ cup	dessicated coconut
¼ cup	Grand Marnier
½ pint	strawberries, halved
¼ cup	toasted sliced almonds
½ cup	whipped cream
½ cup	white marshmallows
½ cup	sour cream

Mix marshmallows, strawberries and sour cream together.

Cut pineapple into thin slices and place one-quarter of the slices in the bottom of a glass bowl. Sprinkle with confectioners sugar. Add a layer of banana slices. Then a layer of coconut and the strawberry mixture. Sprinkle with Grand Marnier. Repeat layers of fruits and liqueur.

Top with whipped cream and garnish with toasted almonds.

NOTE: This recipe can also be made with kiwi fruit, mango, oranges and brandy. Make sure you keep the same quantities of banana and fresh coconut.

PIP'S FAVORITE ORANGE PAVLOVA

Serves 6

2 tsp.	butter
2 tsp.	cornstarch
3	egg whites
¾ cup	granulated sugar
½ tsp.	vanilla
½ tsp.	white vinegar
1 tsp.	cornstarch
	Pinch salt
	Grated zest of 1 orange
1 cup	whipping cream
1 tbsp.	Grand Marnier (optional)
	Fruit for garnish (mandarin orange segments, strawberries or raspberries)
	Toasted almonds for garnish

Preheat oven to 320°F. (160°C).

Grease a pie plate with butter and sprinkle with cornstarch.

Whip egg whites until soft peaks form. Add half the sugar, the vanilla, vinegar, cornstarch and salt. Beat until soft peaks form.

Fold in remaining sugar and the orange zest. Mound mixture on prepared pie plate. Bake for 1 hour. Remove from oven and cool. Whip the cream with Grand Marnier. Spread whipped cream over cooled pie. Garnish.

BARBECUED BANANA SPLITS WITH CHOCOLATE SAUCE

Serves 6

6 tbsp.	dark rum
6	bananas
6	scoops vanilla ice cream
⅓ cup	crushed mixed unsalted nuts, toasted

CHOCOLATE SAUCE

8 oz.	semisweet chocolate
1	egg yolk
¼ cup	cream
1 tbsp.	granulated sugar

To make chocolate sauce, melt chocolate in top of double boiler over simmering water. In a bowl, beat egg yolk, cream and sugar. Stir into melted chocolate, beating constantly until smooth. Keep warm.

Place rum in a cook's syringe. Inject rum under the skin of each banana in several places. Place bananas, still in their skins, on barbecue grill. Cook for 8 minutes, turning 3 or 4 times. Don't worry if the skins turn black.

Peel hot bananas and cut in half lengthwise. Set 2 halves on each plate. Top with a scoop of ice cream and chocolate sauce. Garnish with toasted nuts and serve immediately.

CITRUS PARFAIT

Serves 8

	Zest of 1 lemon, sliced finely
1/4 cup	Cointreau or Grand Marnier
	Juice of 3 lemons
1/4 cup	grapefruit juice
3	eggs, separated
1 cup	granulated sugar
	Pinch cream of tartar
	Pinch salt
2 cups	whipping cream
2 tbsp.	granulated sugar
	Toasted almond slivers for garnish

Place lemon zest in a glass dish. Add orange liqueur and set aside.

In top of a double boiler over simmering water, combine lemon juice, grapefruit juice, egg yolks and half the sugar. Cook, stirring with a wooden spoon, until mixture is well blended and begins to thicken. Do not boil.

Remove from heat and set pan in cold water to stop cooking. Stir for a few minutes, then transfer to a large bowl and let cool.

In another bowl, beat together egg whites, cream of tartar and salt until soft peaks form. Beat in remaining sugar, a little at a time, until stiff peaks form. Carefully fold egg white mixture into cooled lemon and grapefruit mixture.

In a chilled bowl, beat cream until soft peaks form. Beat in sugar slowly until peaks become firm. Fold cream into lemon and egg white mixture.

Spoon mixture into 8 chilled parfait glasses. Cover with plastic wrap and place in freezer for 2 to 3 hours. To serve parfait, remove from freezer. Drain lemon zest. Garnish each parfait glass with lemon zest and toasted almond slivers.

GINGER ICE CREAM

Serves 4

3	eggs, separated
1/4 cup	granulated sugar
	Pinch salt
1 cup	light cream
1/4 cup	drained preserved ginger or glacé ginger
1/4 cup	Midori (melon) liqueur or Grand Marnier
1 tbsp.	granulated sugar
1 cup	whipping cream

In a bowl, combine egg yolks, sugar and a pinch of salt. Beat until fluffy and pale yellow.

Scald cream in a saucepan. Let cool. While cream is cooling, place ginger in a blender. Process to a smooth paste. Add the liqueur and blend again. Set aside. Pour the cooled cream into the egg yolk mixture in a fine steady stream, beating continually.

Transfer the egg yolk mixture to the top of a double boiler over simmering water. Cook, stirring occasionally, over moderate heat until mixture thickens and coats the back of a spoon, about 5 to 8 minutes. Do not let it boil.

When custard has thickened, remove the saucepan from the double boiler and place its base in cold water to stop the cooking. Stir for a minute or two until the mixture cools, then add ginger mixture.

In a separate bowl, whip egg whites with sugar until soft peaks form. Fold gently into the ginger custard. Whip the cream and fold into the egg mixture. Mix well.

Place mixture in a pan and freeze. Stir a couple of times in the first hour with a fork to prevent ice crystals forming. Freeze 4 to 6 hours, or until set.

CHOCOLATE AND CRÈME DE MENTHE PIE

Makes one pie

8 oz.	chocolate-coated wheatmeal biscuits
¼ cup	unsalted butter, melted
¼ cup	water
1	envelope unflavored gelatin
3	eggs, separated
½ cup	granulated sugar
½ cup	crème de menthe
¾ cup	whipping cream
2 oz.	semisweet chocolate, grated
9-inch	springform pan

Put biscuits in a plastic bag and crush well with a rolling pin, or process in batches in a food processor.

Put the crumbs in a deep bowl. Add butter and blend well. Spread the mixture in the bottom of the greased springform pan. Chill for 1 hour.

To make filling, put water in the top of a double boiler. Sprinkle gelatin over water and mix well. Place over a pan of simmering water and heat until gelatin is dissolved. Stir and remove from heat.

In a bowl, beat egg yolks with half the sugar. Add gradually to the gelatin, beating until ingredients are well mixed.

Place over simmering water again and cook, stirring with a wooden spoon, until the mixture is thick enough to coat the back of the spoon, about 5 minutes. Do not boil.

Remove from heat and stir in crème de menthe. Pour into a mixing bowl and chill for about 45 minutes, or until mixture begins to set. Stir occasionally.

Beat egg whites with remaining sugar until soft peaks form. Fold egg whites into chilled crème de menthe mixture. Whip cream, then fold into mixture.

Place a waxed paper collar around top of springform pan. Pour filling into pan. Chill for several hours, or until set. Remove collar. Just before serving, sprinkle with grated chocolate.

FRESH BERRY ICE

Serves 6

1 pint	fresh strawberries
1 pint	fresh raspberries
½ cup	granulated sugar
½ cup	water
	Juice of 1 orange
	Juice of 1 lemon
¼ cup	Cointreau (optional)

Wash and hull the berries and place them in a blender. Combine sugar and water in a saucepan and heat, stirring continuously, until sugar has dissolved. Add sugared water to blender; then add orange and lemon juice and blend until mixture is puréed. Stir in liqueur.

Pour into wine glasses and cover with plastic wrap. Freeze for 3 or 4 hours. Do not freeze any longer or the ice may become too hard.

BISCUIT TORTONI

Serves 6

3	eggs, separated
½ cup	confectioners sugar
½ cup	crushed coconut macaroons
½ cup	toasted slivered almonds
¼ cup	finely chopped glacé red cherries
2 tbsp.	Grand Marnier
1 cup	whipping cream
8 oz.	semisweet chocolate, grated

Beat egg yolks with sugar until smooth and thick. Stir in crushed macaroons, half the slivered almonds, the cherries and Grand Marnier.

In another bowl, beat egg whites until stiff. Fold carefully into macaroon mixture.

In a third bowl, whip the cream until stiff. Fold gently into macaroon mixture.

Spread half the macaroon mixture in a flat pan and spread evenly. Cover with a thick layer of grated chocolate. Top with remaining macaroon mixture. Sprinkle with remaining slivered almonds.

Cover with foil and freeze in a plastic container 4 to 5 hours, or until firm. Cut into slices and serve.

AVOCADO FOOL

Serves 6

3	large avocados
	Juice of 2 limes or lemons
2 tbsp.	icing sugar
½ cup	whipping cream
½ cup	pistachio nuts, blanched and chopped
1	kiwi fruit, peeled and sliced into 6 pieces

Peel avocados. Remove pits and dice flesh. In a blender, combine lime juice and icing sugar. Blend for 30 seconds. Add avocado and blend until smooth. Pour into a large bowl.

Beat the cream until soft peaks form. Fold cream gently into the avocado mixture.

Divide the avocado mixture among 6 champagne glasses. To serve, sprinkle with pistachio nuts and top with a slice of kiwi fruit.

Glossary of Terms

BASTE – To moisten ingredients by brushing them with a liquid while they are cooking

BEAT – To stir or whip continually with a vigorous motion

BLANCH – To plunge in salted boiling water for a short time, then place under cold running water

BLEND – To mix thoroughly, either by hand or in electric blender

COAT – To cover with a thin layer

CUBE – To chop food in squares of equal size

DICE – To cut in smaller cubes

DISSOLVE – To mix a dry substance with a liquid until it is absorbed

DRIZZLE – To pour in a fine steady stream over food

FOLD – To combine ingredients gently, being careful not to beat

GARNISH – To decorate food

GREASE – To make oily by rubbing on fat or butter

MARINADE – A liquid in which ingredients are soaked for a period of time to enhance their flavors and tenderize meat

MARINATE – To place food in a marinade and leave it

MIX – To combine ingredients

PURÉE – To make solid ingredients into a smooth liquid, usually with the aid of a blender or food processor

SAUTÉ – To fry lightly in oil or butter

THICKEN – To make a smooth paste by adding water to cornstarch, then stirring it into a hot liquid

TOSS – To mix ingredients gently by using a fork or spoon

WHIP – To beat rapidly to change the consistency

ZEST – Fine shavings of a citrus fruit made by grating the peel

Glossary of Ingredients

CAPER – A pungent pickled bud of a bramble-like shrub, capers are available bottled in gourmet sections of supermarkets or in delicatessens.

CARDAMON – A spice often used in Indian cooking, but also found in the food of Saudi Arabia, Scandinavia, Sri Lanka and Central America. Cardamon pods have a sweet but spicy flavor.

CHINESE HOISIN SAUCE – A sauce used in Chinese cooking and made from sugar, vinegar, soya bean, water, salt, flour, red rice, chili and other spices.

CHIVES – A herb related to the onion family but with a very delicate flavor. Chives should never be cooked, but are popular as a garnish for egg and cheese dishes as well as on salads and buttered boiled potatoes.

CORIANDER – A herb closely related to dill, caraway, fennel and anise. Often used as a garnish. Ground coriander is also available.

CUMIN – A herb resembling caraway. Available ground, but it is best to buy the seeds and grind them as you need them. Often an ingredient in Indian curry.

DILL – An aromatic herb especially used in pickling gherkins and onions. Excellent in cream sauces and soups or with salad dressings.

FENNEL – A herb with an aniseed flavor, often used in fish dishes and salads.

FETA CHEESE – A Greek semisoft curd cheese.

FIVE SPICE POWDER – A blend of Chinese spices: star anise, cinnamon, cloves, fennel and pepper.

GARAM MASALA – A mixture of hot spices used in Indian and Pakistani cooking. It is available on the spice rack of most specialty stores.

MACADAMIA NUT – A round, hard, oily nut grown in Australia and Hawaii.

OREGANO – A herb widely used in Italy for flavoring sauces.

PAPPADUMS – Thin, crisp discs, often flavored with spices, found in Indian grocery stores. They need only a quick frying before serving.

PINE NUT – A small, pale nut used specifically in making Italian pesto. Often available in Italian grocery stores.

PORT SALUT CHEESE – A semihard yellow cheese with a distinctive reddish rind. It has a fairly bland taste when young, but as it ages the flavor becomes more pronounced.

RICOTTA CHEESE – A soft, bland Italian cheese, it is one of the main ingredients in lasagna and is also good in desserts.

ROMANO CHEESE – A hard Italian cheese resembling Parmesan. Grated, it keeps longer than Parmesan and has a more subtle taste.

ROSEMARY – A popular seasoning in England, France and Italy, where it is used primarily with meat, especially lamb. Rosemary must be used sparingly as it has a very strong flavor.

ROQUEFORT CHEESE – A crumbly blue French cheese with a wonderful strong flavor.

SAMBAL OELEK – A bottled spice used in Asia, sambal oelek is made from crushed chilies. It can sometimes be used instead of fresh chilies.

SHALLOT – Not as strong as the common onion, shallots can be used in salads and sauces.

SHOYU – Japanese soy sauce, milder in flavor than its Chinese counterpart.

TARRAGON – A herb used in making tarragon vinegar and mustard, and a major ingredient in some French sauces, for example Béarnaise and tartare sauces.

TURMERIC – One of the principal ingredients of Indian curry powder. It has a pronounced flavor and acts as a yellow coloring agent.

WATER CHESTNUTS – A crisp vegetable used in Oriental cooking, found in cans at the supermarket.

Index